STEP-BY-STEP

50 Spectacular Salads

STEP-BY-STEP

50 Spectacular Salads

Steven Wheeler

Photography by Edward Allwright

LORENZ BOOKS

First published in 1994 by Lorenz Books

© Anness Publishing Limited

Lorenz Books is an imprint of Anness Publishing Limited
Boundary Row Studios
1 Boundary Row
London SE1 8HP

ISBN 1 85967 000 8

Distributed in Australia by Treasure Press

Editorial Director: Joanna Lorenz
Series Editor: Lindsay Porter
Designers: Peter Butler, Bob Gordon
Photographer: Edward Allwright
Stylist: Hilary Guy

Printed and bound in Italy by Graphicom S.r.l., Vicenza

ACKNOWLEDGEMENTS
The author and publishers would like to thank The Oil Merchant, 47 Ashchurch Grove, London
W12 9BU for generously supplying the salads oils used in this book. For mail order enquiries,
telephone 081 740 1335.

MEASUREMENTS
*Three sets of equivalent measurements have been provided in the recipes here, in the following
order: Metric, Imperial and American. It is essential that units of measurement are not mixed
within each recipe. Where conversions result in awkward numbers, these have been rounded for
convenience, but are accurate enough to produce successful results.*

CONTENTS

INTRODUCTION

A well-made salad is almost lyrical in its combination of fresh tastes, textures and colours expressing a particular mood or theme. This book looks at a variety of salad themes and shows that there is more to salads than meets the eye.

Seasonal changes are important and provide a useful lead when you are searching for inspiration. The finest salads begin with one or two ingredients that may catch the attention. If you come across a butter-rich pear, partner it with a handful of toasted pecan nuts, a few leaves of young spinach, and combine with a blue cheese dressing. If a freshly boiled crab takes your fancy, consider the rich flavours of avocado, coriander leaves and lime. Some new potatoes and young lettuce leaves will make it a salad to remember.

Most salads fit into the summer season and are inspired by an abundance of freshness and colour. Summer salads are best eaten out of doors. In autumn and winter we move inside to enjoy the warm flavours of wild mushrooms, duck breast and chicken livers. The richness of these ingredients combines especially well with hearty leaves of oakleaf lettuce, escarole and chicory. Spring sees the arrival of young vegetables and tender salad leaves: corn salad, spinach and rocket. These delicate flavours marry best with simply grilled fish, eggs, ham and chicken. At the rear of this book is a special index linked to ingredients you are most likely to have in store. From it you can decide which salad is most practical to make.

Simplicity is the key to a successful salad. Where two or more ingredients combine, their flavours should marry well together but should also still be individually identifiable. May your salads bring good health and happiness to your table!

Salad Vegetables

The salad vegetable is any type that earns its keep in a salad by virtue of freshness and flavour. Vegetables for a salad can be raw or lightly cooked. If cooked, they are best served warm or at room temperature to bring out their full flavour. No amount of guesswork can replace a sound knowledge of which vegetables partner most effectively.

Celery is a useful salad vegetable and is grown year round for its robust earthy flavour. The crisp stems should be neither stringy nor tough. Celery partners well with cooked ham, apple and walnut in Waldorf Salad. It also belongs with Swiss cheese, chicken and tongue.

Bulb or Florence fennel has a strong aniseed flavour and looks like a squat head of celery. From its centre it puts forth soft green fronds that can be chopped and used as a herb. Because the flavour of the vegetable can be dominant, it may be blanched in boiling water for 6 minutes before use in a salad.

The turnip is grown for its tender tops and clean white root. When young, the bulbous root has a peppery sweetness. Its flavour marries well with creamed horseradish and caraway seed and is an excellent partner to cold roast beef.

The cucumber is a common salad ingredient and turns up, invited or not, in salad bowls everywhere. The robust quality of this vegetable is best appreciated in strongly flavoured salads.

Fresh garlic is essential to the cooking of South America, Asia and the Mediterranean. Strong to taste, garlic promotes good health and a vigorous appetite. To moderate the strength of fresh garlic, store crushed cloves in olive oil and use the oil sparingly in salad dressings.

The spring onion (scallion) has a milder flavour than the common onion and gives a gentle bite to many popular salads. The mature variety has a stronger flavour than younger onions.

Mushrooms provide a rich tone to many salads and are eaten both raw and cooked. The oyster mushroom, which grows wild in late summer and autumn, has a fine flavour and texture. This and other wild varieties are often cultivated in a semi-wild environment to meet consumer demand. White and brown button mushrooms combine well with fresh garlic, herbs and butter.

Tomatoes play an important part in salads and are valued for flavour and colour. Dwarf varieties usually ripen more quickly than large ones and tend to have a better flavour.

There are three main varieties of onion that are suited to salads. The strongest, pictured here, is the small brown onion. It should be chopped finely and used sparingly. Less strong are the Spanish and vidalia onions, which may be coarsely chopped.

The avocado pear has a smooth buttery flesh when ripe and is an asset to many salads, of which Guacamole is perhaps the best known. Avocados are rich in calories and are a good source of potassium and B group vitamins.

Before sweetcorn is fully grown, the baby cobs can be lightly cooked or eaten raw and should be served warm or at room temperature with other young vegetables.

Courgettes can be bitter to taste and are usually cooked before being combined with other young vegetables. Smooth in texture when cooked, they marry wonderfully with tomatoes, aubergines, peppers and onions.

Carrots should be young, slender and sweet to taste. Either cooked or raw, they bring flavour and colour to a salad. Raw carrots are a valuable source of vitamin A and are rich in minerals.

The varieties of green bean are too numerous to mention here, but they all have their merits as salad vegetables. To appreciate the sweet flavour of green beans, cook them for no longer than 6 minutes. Properly cooked green beans should squeak between the teeth when bitten into.

Left: *Almost any vegetable can be used in a salad, either raw or lightly cooked. You will only need a limited number of ingredients to create a successful salad if you choose complementary flavours.*

Selecting Fruit

The contents of the fruit bowl offers endless possibilities for sweet and savoury salads. Sweet fruit salads are probably the best known, although in these individual fruits are inclined to get lost in a multi-coloured muddle where varieties merge into one flavour. When preparing a fruit salad, aim to combine both flavours and colours in such a way that the dish looks and tastes as appetizing as possible. When choosing fruit, make sure that it tastes as good as it looks. If fruit is fresh and ripe, it has every reason to taste good in a salad.

A knowledge of which fruits combine most effectively is essential if you are going to make your own salad combinations. The flavour of ripe pineapple, for example, combines best with strawberries, lychees and oranges; other tropical fruits belong with pineapple, but few bring out its sweetness as well. Pineapples are available all year round, but are best in May and June. Ripe pineapples resist firm pressure in the hand and have a sweet smell.

Bananas bring a special richness to fruit salads, although their distinct flavour can often interfere with more delicate fruit. Lightly grilled, bananas are delicious with a salad of barbecued chicken, bacon, sweetcorn and tart leaves of watercress. Under-ripe yellow bananas are not easily digested: make sure that the skin is mottled brown but free from bruising.

A bunch of grapes on the table is almost a dessert in itself. Large Muscat varieties, whose season runs from late summer to autumn, are the most coveted and also the most expensive. When thoroughly chilled and served with a frozen granita of Muscat wine, Muscat grapes make an impressive dessert.

When in season, oranges have a bright challenging flavour. Citrus fruits are at their best during winter when individual fruits feel heavy for their size. Oranges are best segmented and added to sweet and savoury salads. Their sharpness balances the richness of many fish salads.

Unusual tropical fruits import character to exotic salads. The visually dramatic pithaya offers little flavour, but is appreciated for its luscious black and white interior. Some varieties of this South American cactus fruit have a crimson-pink flesh.

The mango and the pawpaw or papaya are two fruits that lend themselves to exotic salads. Mangoes show a red blush when ripe. Pawpaws become yellow-green and yield to firm pressure in the hand.

Apples and pears grow in temperate climates as far south as Argentina and Cape Town. Both fruits offer a unique flavour to sweet and savoury salads. Ripe pears taste especially good with strong blue cheese and toasted pecan nuts in a savoury salad. Apples find favour in a Waldorf Salad with ham, celery and walnuts.

Melons grow in abundance from mid to late summer and provide a resource of freshness and flavour. Pictured here is water melon, the largest variety with the most succulent flavour; and galia and charentais, which have a sweeter, more penetrating fragrance. Melon is at its most delicious served icy cold.

The raspberry is a much-coveted soft fruit that partners well with ripe mango, passion fruit and strawberries.

The strawberry, one of the most popular summer fruits, is best eaten at room temperature with sugar and cream.

Wild blackberries are at their best from late summer to autumn when they can be found in hedgerows. Cultivated varieties are available but have a less dramatic flavour. The blackberry, a member of the rose family, is delicious served with a granita of rose water.

Blueberries are everyone's favourite fruit stirred into pancakes, but these tight-skinned berries are also delicious in an unusual salad with orange and lavender meringue. Blueberries enjoy the sharpness of fresh oranges. Cultivated blueberries are sold from spring to autumn, but wild varieties are the most flavoursome.

Right: *Fresh fruits can be used in both sweet and savoury salads. Ensure they are ripe and in peak condition.*

Salad Leaves

Batavian endive
The Batavian endive has a bitter flavour similar to escarole but a slightly sweeter, softer taste. It is suited to most salads and stands up to a well-flavoured dressing.

Cos lettuce
The cos or romaine lettuce, which originated on the Greek island of Cos, has a robust slightly bitter flavour. Cos is the preferred salad leaf for Caesar salad.

Escarole
Escarole is a robust green salad leaf that, like curly endive and chicory, has a bitter flavour. It is best during the winter months and is usually served with a sweet dressing.

Frisée lettuce
Frisée or curly endive is a member of the chicory family. It has a clean bitter taste that combines well with sweeter salad leaves.

Iceberg lettuce
The tightly packed iceberg lettuce has a crisp texture, with little flavour of its own. It is suited to fine shredding and combines well with strong dressings and other salad leaves.

Lamb's lettuce
Lamb's lettuce or corn salad grows year round in small fragile shoots. These are eaten whole and have a mild sweet flavour.

Little gem
Little gem or sucrine is a small, sweet compact lettuce similar in flavour to cos or romaine. Its well-formed leaves are inclined to keep longer than those of many other lettuce varieties.

Lollo biondo
Lollo biondo or green lollo is a loose-leaved lettuce with a curly edge. It has a mild flavour and belongs with stronger-tasting lettuce leaves.

Lollo rosso
Lollo rosso or red lollo is a mild-flavoured lettuce with a curly edge. This loose-leaved variety is appreciated for its purple-red tint.

Oakleaf lettuce
The broad wavy leaves of oakleaf or feuille de chêne are tinted a purple-brown. Its dark colour and mild taste combine well with the bitter leaves of escarole and curly endive.

Rocket (arugula)
Rocket (arugula) has a peppery taste of lemon and is often combined with milder leaves to add flavour and zest. Rocket leaves keep well when immersed in cold water.

Spinach
Young spinach leaves, used in many salads, are appreciated for their rich sweet flavour. If the leaves are large, the stems should be removed before washing.

Watercress
Watercress, which has a tart peppery taste, is a member of the mustard family. Its strong flavour combines especially well with eggs, fish and grilled meats.

lollo rosso

Batavian endive

frisée lettuce

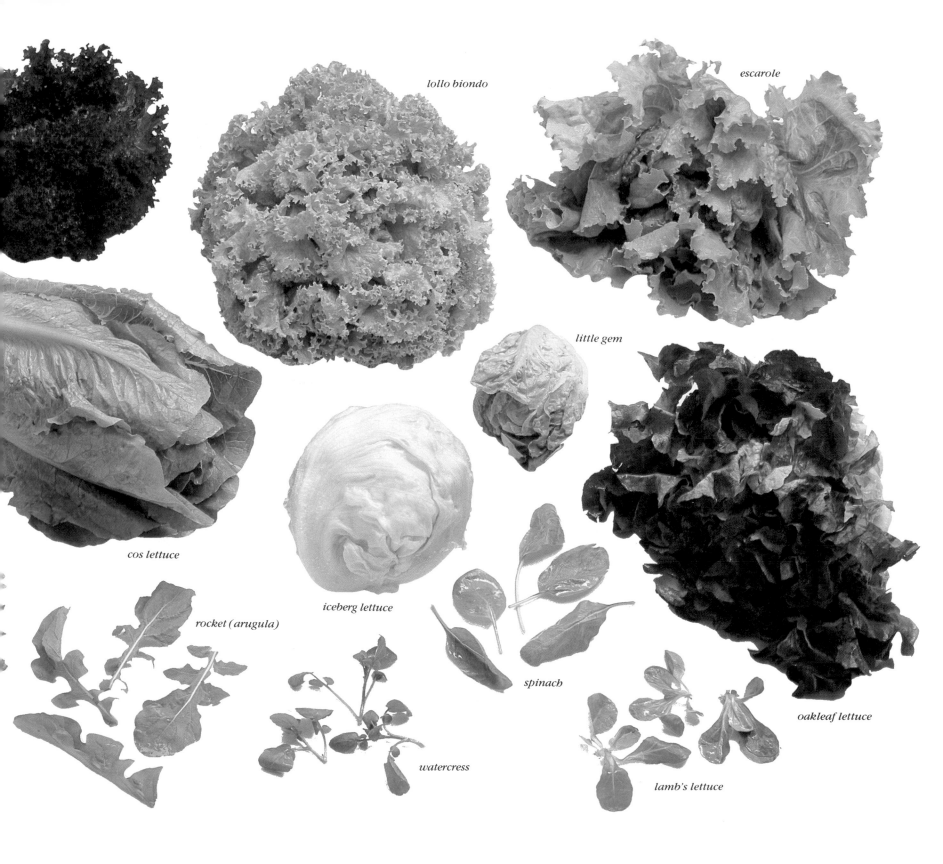

lollo biondo

escarole

little gem

cos lettuce

iceberg lettuce

rocket (arugula)

spinach

oakleaf lettuce

watercress

lamb's lettuce

Dressing Ingredients

The best-dressed salads are those that allow individual ingredients to taste of themselves. Too many salads are ruined with badly made dressings in which vinegar dominates. An excess of vinegar drowns the quality of a salad and also plays havoc with any wine that is served with it.

Oil is the main ingredient of most dressings and provides an important richness to salads. Most of the salad oil used today is taken from the seed or kernel of the sunflower, safflower, groundnut (peanut) or soya bean. These neutral oils have little flavour and are ideally used as a background for stronger oils. Sesame, walnut and hazelnut oils are the strongest and should be used sparingly. Olive oil is prized for its clarity of flavour and clean richness. The most significant producers of olive oil are Italy, France, Spain and Greece. These and other countries produce three main grades of olive oil: estate-grown extra-virgin olive oil, for which olives have been hand-picked and cold-pressed to give an individual flavour; virgin olive oil, for which olives have been mechanically picked and often warmed before pressing to extract a higher percentage of oil; and semi-fine olive oil, of an ordinary standard best suited to high-temperature frying. Many extra-virgin olive oils compare with château-bottled wines. They tend to be expensive and reflect individual character and taste. It is best to reflect the nationality of a salad by using an oil of the same country.

Garlic oil

Garlic oil is made by steeping 4–5 crushed cloves of garlic in a neutral-flavoured oil. The oil can then be used to impart a gentle garlic taste to salad dressings of many kinds. Garlic oil is also useful when frying bread croûtons.

Olive oils

French olive oils are subtly flavoured and provide a well-balanced lightness to dressings. The golden oil featured here has a sweet fruity flavour and is suited to the foods of southern France.

Greek olive oils are typically strong in character. They are often green with a thick texture and are unsuitable for mayonnaise.

Italian olive oils are noted for their vigorous Mediterranean flavours and suggest grassy herbs – often a prickly taste of black pepper. Tuscan oils are noted for their well-rounded spicy flavour and are often green in colour. Sicilian oils tend to be lighter in texture, although they are often more strongly flavoured than Tuscan oils.

Spanish olive oils are typically fruity and often have a nutty quality with a pleasant bitterness.

Nut oils

Hazelnut and walnut oils are valued for their strong nutty flavour. Tasting richly of the nuts from which they are pressed, both are usually blended with neutral oils for salad dressings.

Seed oils

Groundnut (peanut) oil and sunflower oil are valued by many cooks for their clean neutral flavour. These and other seed oils – safflower, soya and grapeseed – are used in conjunction with stronger oils. Corn oil is considered to be too sweet and cloying for salad use.

Vinegars

White wine vinegar is probably the most popular type for salad dressings, but it should be used in moderation to balance the richness of an oil. There are many other vinegars from which to choose; however, a good-quality white wine vinegar will serve most purposes.

Capers

Capers are the pickled flower buds of a bush native to the Mediterranean. Their strong sharp flavour is well suited to richly flavoured salads. Smaller, tightly packed capers are more intensely flavoured than larger varieties.

Lemon and lime juice

The juice of lemons and limes is used to impart a clean acidity to oil dressings. Both have a similar strength to vinegar and should be used in moderation.

Mustard

Mustard has a tendency to bring out the flavour of other ingredients. It acts as an emulsifier in dressings and allows oil and vinegar to merge for a short period of time. Where possible French, German and English mustards should be used for salads of the same nationality.

Olives

Black and green olives belong in salads that take their flavour from the sun. Black olives are generally sweeter than green ones, although many green olives are treated with sugar and sometimes lemon juice to encourage their flavour.

Italian olive oil

Spanish olive o

lemon

Italian olive oil

safflower oil

hazelnut oil

walnut oil

groundnut oil

French olive oil

Italian olive oil

garlic oil

limes

olives

capers

mustard

white wine vinegar

Using Herbs

For as long as salads draw on the qualities of fresh produce, sweet herbs have an important part to play in providing individual character and flavour. The word fresh is used here to imply that salad ingredients are alive with flavour. When herbs are used in a salad, they should be as full of life as the salad leaves they accompany. Dried herbs are no substitute for fresh ones and should be kept for stews and casseroles. Salad herbs are distinguished by their ability to release flavour without lengthy cooking. Most salad herbs belong

finely chopped in salad dressings and marinades, while the robust flavours of rosemary, thyme and fennel branches can be used on the barbecue to impart a smoky herb flavour to meat and fish. Ideally salad herbs should be picked just before use, but if you cannot use them immediately, keep them in water to retain their freshness. Parsley, mint and coriander will keep for up to a week in this way if also covered with a plastic bag and placed in the refrigerator.

Garden mint is the most common mint variety. Others

include spearmint, with its jagged leaf edge, and apple mint which has a round leaf shape. The flavour of mint is unusual because it distinguishes and cleanses other flavours instead of merging with them. Mint is widely used in Greek and Middle Eastern salads, such as Tzatziki and Tabbouleh, to provide a clean refreshing flavour.

Basil, a summer herb related to mint, is remarkable for its fresh pungent flavour. Its aniseed-clove fragrance is released by rubbing a few leaves in the hand. It is the signature of many Italian dishes, but appears throughout the Mediterranean in a variety of salad dishes. Dried basil is no substitute for the fresh herb.

Fresh thyme is an asset to salads that feature rich, earthy flavours. Native to southern Europe, it has a penetrating minty lemon flavour. The two main varieties are broad-leaf English and narrow-leaf French thyme. Both are used in conjunction with parsley, garlic, marjoram and lavender to create Mediterranean flavours.

Flat- and curly-leaf parsley are both grown for their fresh green flavour — reminiscent of carrot, celery and caraway. Flat-leaf or continental parsley is said to have a stronger taste and is certainly

easier to chop. More than just a garnish, freshly chopped parsley is used by the handful in salads and salad dressings, especially those that contain garlic. Dried parsley is not suitable for salads.

Chives are a member of the onion family and have a mild onion flavour. The slender green stems, which grow wild in wet meadows, belong with the scent of summer garlic. Chives produce a soft magenta flower which is edible. Freeze-dried chives are available, but are not recommended for salad use.

Fresh lavender is native to the rocky hills of the Mediterranean and has been enjoyed since Greek and Roman times for its soothing fragrance. All lavender is edible and combines naturally with thyme, garlic, marjoram, honey and orange. As a marinade, this combination is delicious with a grilled chicken salad. Lavender's association with orange enables us to enjoy it in a fruit salad of blueberry and meringue.

Although it is not technically a herb, the sweet-scented rose can be used to flavour fresh fruit salads. The blackberry and raspberry are members of the rose family, an association that allows their characters to mingle.

Left: *Flavourful additions to salads include (clockwise from top left) thyme, flat-leaf parsley, chives, lavender, rose petals, mint and basil.*

Using Spices

Spices are the aromatic seasonings found in the seed, bark, fruit and sometimes flowers of certain plants and trees. The value of spices has been appreciated in Europe since the Arabs first monopolized the Eastern spice trade over 3,000 years ago. Prices remained high until ocean trade was established by Britain in the seventeenth century. Today we still value spices for their warm inviting flavours, and thankfully their price is relatively low. The flavour of spice is contained in the volatile oils of the seed, bark or fruit; so, like herbs, spices should be used as fresh as possible. Whole spices keep better than ground ones, which tend to lose their freshness in 3–4 months.

Not all spices are suitable for salad making, although many allow us to explore the flavours of other cultures. The recipes in this book use curry spices – coriander, cumin, cardamom, cinnamon, chilli and turmeric – in moderation so as not to spoil the delicate salad flavours. The moderate use of Indian spices is often found in French cooking when spices are employed with respect for underlying flavour.

Pepper, the most popular spice used in the West, features in the cooking of almost every nation. Freshly ground pepper serves to excite the taste buds, thus increasing our awareness of taste sensation. Pepper is the fruit of a tropical vine, native to the forests of monsoon Asia, but today it is grown as far west as Madagascar. The berries are picked in clusters when green, and drying develops their black colour. Black peppercorns have the mildest flavour and should always be freshly ground in a mill. Both salt and pepper should be added to a salad after it is dressed.

Cayenne pepper, also known as chilli powder, is the dried and finely ground fruit of the hot chilli. It has a similar effect on the taste buds as the peppercorn and is an important seasoning in South American cooking. Cayenne pepper is used in preference to black or white pepper when seasoning fish and shellfish. If chilli powder is too hot, it can be blended with mild paprika. Care should be taken when using cayenne pepper – a little goes a long way.

Celery salt is a combination of celery seed and salt. It is usually sold ready-made, although you can make your own by pounding equal volumes of celery seed and fine salt in a pestle and mortar. If celery seed is not available, lovage seed, which has a strong celery taste, can be substituted. Celery salt is most often used when seasoning vegetables, in particular carrots with which celery has a strong association. Care should be taken not to over-salt when trying to impart a celery flavour .

Right: A little spice goes a long way in salad making. Spices include (clockwise from top left) celery salt, caraway seeds, curry paste, saffron, black peppercorns, cayenne pepper.

Caraway seeds are widely used in German, Alsatian and Austrian cooking and feature strongly in many Jewish dishes. The small ribbed seeds are similar in appearance and taste to cumin and have a savoury-sweet quality, thought to aid digestion. The flavour of caraway combines especially well with German mustard in a dressing for Frankfurter Salad.

Prepared curry paste is the best medium in which to preserve the flavour of Indian spices; it keeps better than blended powder, which is inclined to go stale. Madras paste has a good medium strength. Curry spices combine especially well in dressings and show off the sweet qualities of fish and shellfish.

Saffron, the world's most expensive spice, is made from the dried red-orange stigma of a purple-flowering crocus traditionally grown in Spain. Real saffron has a tobacco-rich smell and gives a sweet yellow tint to liquids used for cooking. There are many imitations which provide colour without the flavour of the real thing. Saffron can be used in rich creamy dressings and brings out the richness of fresh seafood.

Equipment

Cheese grater
A sturdy cheese grater is widely used by the salad maker for grating hard-boiled eggs, vegetables and the outer zest of citrus fruit.

Food processor
The food processor is useful for mixing and blending salad ingredients. Most have an attachment for slicing and grating large quantities.

Hand whisk
A sturdy hand whisk is useful for combining dressing ingredients smoothly. The best whisks are made of stainless steel and have a secure, hard plastic handle.

Knives
Chopping and paring knives are subject to personal choice and should feel comfortable in the hand. Large chopping knives should be handled with care and respect for their sharpness.

Measuring cups and spoons
Measuring cups and spoons are useful for gauging accurately the volume and corresponding weight of salad ingredients. Spoon measures range from 3 ml/½ tsp to 15 ml/1 tbsp and cups from 50 ml/2 fl oz/¼ cup to 200 ml/ 8 fl oz/1 cup

Mixing bowls
An assortment of glass mixing bowls that fit neatly inside each other are useful for a number of salad preparations.

Salad bowl
A sensibly shaped salad bowl with sloping sides is most practical for tossing salad leaves. Two large spoons are best for serving.

Saucepan
A good stainless-steel saucepan is a sound investment for any cook. The best pans are sold individually rather than as a set. They are expensive but will last a lifetime of simmering, blanching and boiling.

Screw-top jar
A screw-top jar is most practical for making and storing salad dressings. Make sure that the jar has a tight-fitting lid.

salad bowl

saucepan

mixing bowls

cheese grater

hand whisk

knives

measuring cups and spoons

food processor

screw-top jar

The Kitchen Garden

During spring and summer many cooks like to grow their own supply of fresh herbs and salad leaves. A small garden planted in a sunny spot near the kitchen allows you to gather fresh produce as and when you need it. The extent of a kitchen garden can range from a few pots to a growing-bag or an open soil bed. Most cooks enjoy the convenience of a few herbs growing in pots by the window, and may be tempted to raise unusual varieties from seed.

Planting seeds

Every packet of seeds carries instructions for planting. If you are growing herbs and salad leaves for the window sill, you can germinate seeds in partitioned trays and transfer the plants, as they grow, to well-drained pots until they are large enough to be planted in the garden. Regular watering and plenty of sun will ensure an abundance of freshness and flavour. Tomatoes can be grown from seed, but most gardeners prefer to buy young plants. Tomato plants do well in growing-bags on a patio and are best positioned against a south-facing wall. Vegetables such as carrots, radishes, beetroot and turnips are best planted in an open bed of rich soil. Seedlings that grow too close together should be thinned to enable proper development. Young thinnings are delicious in fresh colourful salads.

Growing in pots

If you have only a small garden, salad leaves and herbs can be grown successfully in terracotta pots. Regular watering is important and all pots should allow for drainage. For a constant supply of lettuce, sow seeds at 2-week intervals throughout the summer and pick when needed. In colder weather, herbs and salad leaves should be kept under glass to maximize warmth from the sun. Many herbs enjoy a sunny spot on an inside window ledge.

Picking and storing herbs

When herbs are picked, every effort should be made to keep their flavour intact. In season, bunches of parsley, mint, coriander and chives keep well in water. Covered with a plastic bag, these herbs will keep in the refrigerator for up to a week. Herbs such as thyme, rosemary and lavender are suitable for slow drying in a well-ventilated cupboard. Dried herbs will keep for several months.

Above right: *Seeds can be grown in small trays on the window sill, and then transplanted to individual pots. When large enough, plant them in the garden.*

Right: *Herbs include (clockwise from top right) flat-leaf parsley, lavender, thyme and chives.*

Opposite: *If space is at a premium, salad leaves and herbs can be grown successfully on the window sill.*

Mayonnaise

Mayonnaise is a simple emulsion made with egg yolks and oil. For consistent results, ensure that both egg yolks and oil are at room temperature before combining – around 21°C/70°F. Home-made mayonnaise is made with raw egg yolks and may therefore be considered unsuitable for young children, pregnant mothers and the elderly.

Makes about 300 ml/12 fl oz/1½ cups

INGREDIENTS
2 egg yolks
5 ml/1 tsp French mustard
150 ml/5 fl oz/⅔ cup extra-virgin
   olive oil, French or Italian
150 ml/5 fl oz/⅔ cup groundnut or
   sunflower oil
10 ml/2 tsp white wine vinegar
salt and pepper

1 Place the egg yolks and mustard in a food processor and blend smoothly.

2 Add the olive oil a little at a time while the processor is running. When the mixture is thick, add the remainder of the oil in a slow steady stream.

3 Add the vinegar and season to taste with salt and pepper.

COOK'S TIP

Should mayonnaise separate during blending, add 30 ml/2 tbsp boiling water and beat until smooth. Store mayonnaise in the refrigerator for up to 1 week, sealed in a screw-top jar.

Blue Cheese and Chive Dressing

Blue cheese dressings have a strong robust flavour and are well suited to winter salad leaves: escarole, chicory and radicchio.

Makes about 350 ml/14 fl oz/1¾ cups

INGREDIENTS
75 g/3 oz blue cheese, Stilton, Bleu
   d'Auvergne or Gorgonzola
150 ml/5 fl oz/⅔ cup medium-fat
   plain yogurt
45 ml/3 tbsp olive oil, preferably
   Italian
30 ml/2 tbsp lemon juice
15 ml/1 tbsp chopped fresh chives
black pepper

2 Add the remainder of the yogurt, the olive oil and lemon juice.

1 Remove the rind from the cheese. Place the cheese with a third of the yogurt in a mixing bowl and combine smoothly with a wooden spoon.

3 Stir in the chives and season to taste with freshly ground black pepper.

French Dressing

French vinaigrette is the most widely used salad dressing and is appreciated for its simplicity and style. For the best flavour, use the finest extra-virgin olive oil and go easy on the vinegar.

Makes about 125 ml/4 fl oz/¹/₂ cup

INGREDIENTS
90 ml/6 tbsp/¹/₃ cup extra-virgin olive oil, French or Italian
15 ml/1 tbsp white wine vinegar
5 ml/1 tsp French mustard
pinch of caster (superfine) sugar

2 Add the mustard and sugar.

1 Place the olive oil and vinegar in a screw-top jar.

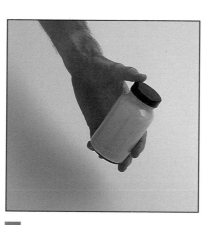

3 Replace the lid and shake well.

French Herb Dressing

The delicate scents of fresh herbs combine especially well in a French dressing. Toss with a simple green salad and serve with good cheese and wine.

Makes about 125 ml/4 fl oz/¹/₂ cup

INGREDIENTS
60 ml/4 tbsp extra-virgin olive oil, French or Italian
30 ml/2 tbsp groundnut or sunflower oil
15 ml/1 tbsp lemon juice
60 ml/4 tbsp finely chopped fresh herbs: parsley, chives, tarragon and marjoram
pinch of caster (superfine) sugar

2 Add the lemon juice, herbs and sugar.

1 Place the olive and groundnut oil in a screw-top jar.

3 Replace the lid and shake well.

COOK'S TIP
Liquid dressings that contain extra-virgin olive oil should be stored at room temperature. Refrigeration can cause them to solidify.

Avocado, Crab and Coriander Salad

The sweet richness of crab combines especially well with ripe avocado, fresh coriander and tomato.

Serves 4

Ingredients

700 g/1½ lb small new potatoes
1 sprig fresh mint
900 g/2 lb boiled crabs, or 275 g/10 oz
   frozen crab meat
1 Batavian endive or butterhead
   lettuce
175 g/6 oz lamb's lettuce or young
   spinach
1 large ripe avocado, peeled and
   sliced
175 g/6 oz cherry tomatoes
salt, pepper and nutmeg

Dressing

75 ml/5 tbsp olive oil, preferably
   Tuscan
15 ml/1 tbsp lime juice
45 ml/3 tbsp chopped fresh coriander
½ tsp caster (superfine) sugar

crab

avocado

cherry
tomatoes

mint

lamb's
lettuce

coriander

new potatoes

1 Scrape or peel the potatoes. Cover with water, add a good pinch of salt and a sprig of mint. Bring to the boil and simmer for 20 minutes. Drain, cover and keep warm until needed.

2 Remove the legs and claws from each crab. Crack these open with the back of a chopping knife and then remove the white meat.

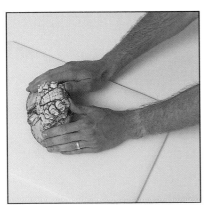

3 Turn the crab on its back and push the rear leg section away with the thumb and forefinger of each hand. Remove the flesh from inside the shell.

4 Discard the soft gills ('dead men's fingers'): the crab uses these gills to filter impurities in its diet. Apart from these and the shell, everything else is edible – white and dark meat.

5 Split the central body section open with a knife and remove the white and dark flesh with a pick or skewer.

COOK'S TIP

Young crabs offer the sweetest meat, but are more fiddly to prepare than older, larger ones. The hen crab carries more flesh than the cock which is considered to have a better overall flavour. The cock crab, shown here, is identified by his narrow apron flap at the rear. The hen has a broad flap under which she carries her eggs. Frozen crab meat is a good alternative to fresh and retains much of its original sweetness.

6 Combine the dressing ingredients in a screw-top jar and shake. Wash and spin the lettuces, then dress them. Distribute between 4 plates. Top with avocado, crab, tomatoes and warm new potatoes. Season with salt, pepper and freshly grated nutmeg and serve.

Swiss Cheese, Chicken and Tongue Salad with Apple and Celery

The rich sweet flavours of this salad marry well with the tart peppery nature of watercress. A minted lemon dressing combines to freshen the overall effect. Serve with warm new potatoes.

Serves 4

INGREDIENTS
2 free-range chicken breasts, skin and
 bone removed
½ chicken stock cube
225 g/8 oz sliced ox tongue or ham,
 6 mm/¼ in thick
225 g/8 oz Gruyère (Swiss) cheese
1 lollo rosso lettuce
1 butterhead or Batavian endive
 lettuce
1 bunch watercress
2 green-skinned apples, cored and
 sliced
3 stalks celery, sliced
60 ml/4 tbsp sesame seeds, toasted
salt, pepper and nutmeg

DRESSING
75 ml/5 tbsp groundnut or sunflower
 oil
5 ml/1 tsp sesame oil
45 ml/3 tbsp lemon juice
10 ml/2 tsp chopped fresh mint
3 drops Tabasco sauce

2 To make the dressing, measure the two oils, lemon juice, mint and Tabasco sauce into a screw-top jar and shake. Cut the chicken, tongue and cheese into fine strips. Moisten with a little dressing and set aside.

3 Wash and spin the salad leaves, combine with the apple and celery, and dress. Distribute between 4 large plates. Pile the chicken, tongue and cheese in the centre, scatter with toasted sesame seeds, season with salt, pepper and freshly grated nutmeg and serve.

1 Place the chicken breasts in a shallow saucepan, cover with 300 ml/10 fl oz water, add the ½ stock cube and bring to the boil. Put the lid on the pan and simmer for 15 minutes. Drain, reserving the stock for another occasion, then cool the chicken under cold running water.

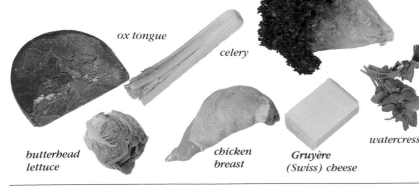

ox tongue

celery

lollo rosso lettuce

butterhead lettuce

chicken breast

Gruyère (Swiss) cheese

watercress

Chicken Liver, Bacon and Tomato Salad

Warm salads are especially welcome during the autumn months when the evenings are growing shorter and cooler. Try this rich salad with sweet spinach and bitter leaves of frisée lettuce.

Serves 4

INGREDIENTS
225 g/8 oz young spinach, stems removed
1 frisée lettuce
105 ml/7 tbsp groundnut or sunflower oil
175 g/6 oz rindless unsmoked bacon, cut into strips
75 g/3 oz day-old bread, crusts removed and cut into short fingers
450 g/1 lb chicken livers
125 g/4 oz cherry tomatoes
salt and pepper

I Wash and spin the salad leaves. Place in a salad bowl. Heat 60 ml/4 tbsp of the oil in a large frying-pan (skillet). Add the bacon and cook for 3–4 minutes or until crisp and brown. Remove the bacon with a slotted spoon and drain on a piece of kitchen paper (paper towel).

2 To make the croûtons, fry the bread in the bacon-flavoured oil, tossing until crisp and golden. Drain on kitchen paper.

3 Heat the remaining 45 ml/3 tbsp of oil in the frying-pan, add the chicken livers and fry briskly for 2–3 minutes. Turn the livers out over the salad leaves, add the bacon, croûtons and tomatoes. Season, toss and serve.

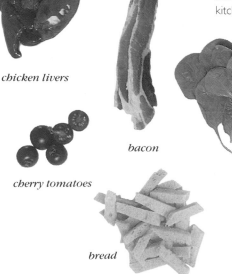

chicken livers

bacon

spinach

cherry tomatoes

bread

Maryland Salad

Barbecue-grilled chicken, sweetcorn, bacon, banana and watercress combine here in a sensational main-course salad. Serve with jacket potatoes and a knob of butter.

Serves 4

INGREDIENTS
4 boneless free-range chicken breasts
salt and pepper
225 g/8 oz rindless unsmoked bacon
4 sweetcorn cobs
45 ml/3 tbsp soft butter
4 ripe bananas, peeled and halved
4 firm tomatoes, halved
1 escarole or butterhead lettuce
1 bunch watercress

DRESSING
75 ml/5 tbsp groundnut oil
15 ml/1 tbsp white wine vinegar
10 ml/2 tsp maple syrup
10 ml/2 tsp mild mustard

1 Season the chicken breasts, brush with oil and barbecue or grill (broil) for 15 minutes, turning once. Barbecue or grill the bacon for 8–10 minutes or until crisp.

2 Bring a large saucepan of salted water to the boil. Shuck and trim the corn cobs or leave the husks on if you prefer. Boil for 20 minutes. For extra flavour, brush with butter and brown over the barbecue or under the grill. Barbecue or grill the bananas and tomatoes for 6–8 minutes: you can brush these with butter too if you wish.

3 To make the dressing, combine the oil, vinegar, maple syrup and mustard with 15 ml/1 tbsp water in a screw-top jar and shake well.

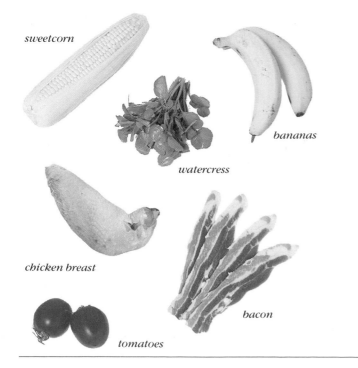

sweetcorn

bananas

watercress

chicken breast

bacon

tomatoes

4 Wash, spin thoroughly and dress the salad leaves.

5 Distribute the salad leaves between 4 large plates. Slice the chicken and arrange over the leaves with the bacon, banana, sweetcorn and tomatoes.

Warm Pasta Salad with Ham, Egg and Asparagus

In the summer months when the weather is hot, try serving your pasta *calda*, as a warm salad. Here it is served with ham, eggs and asparagus. A mustard dressing made from the thick part of asparagus provides a rich accompaniment.

Serves 4

INGREDIENTS
450 g/1 lb asparagus
salt
450 g/1 lb dried tagliatelle
225 g/8 oz sliced cooked ham, 6 mm/
  ¼ in thick, cut into fingers
2 eggs, hard-boiled and sliced
50 g/2 oz Parmesan cheese, shaved

DRESSING
50 g/2 oz cooked potato
75 ml/5 tbsp olive oil, preferably
  Sicilian
15 ml/1 tbsp lemon juice
10 ml/2 tsp Dijon mustard
125 ml/4 fl oz/½ cup vegetable stock

asparagus

tagliatelle

Parmesan cheese

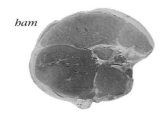
ham

eggs

1 Bring a saucepan of salted water to the boil. Trim and discard the tough woody part of the asparagus. Cut the asparagus in half and boil the thicker halves for 12 minutes. After 6 minutes throw in the tips. Refresh under cold water until warm, then drain.

2 Finely chop 150 g/5 oz of the asparagus middle section. Place in a food processor with the dressing ingredients and process until smooth. Season to taste.

3 Boil the pasta in a large saucepan of salted water according to the packet instructions. Refresh under cold water until warm, and drain. Dress with the asparagus sauce and turn out into 4 pasta plates. Top with the ham, hard-boiled eggs and asparagus tips. Finish with Parmesan cheese.

Minted Egg and Fennel Tabbouleh with Toasted Hazelnuts

Tabbouleh, a Middle Eastern dish of steamed bulghur wheat, is suited to warm-weather picnics.

Serves 4

INGREDIENTS
250 g/9 oz/1¼ cups bulghur wheat
2 eggs
1 bulb fennel
1 bunch spring onions (scallions), chopped
25 g/1 oz sun-dried tomatoes, sliced
45 ml/3 tbsp chopped fresh parsley
30 ml/2 tbsp chopped fresh mint
75 g/3 oz black olives
60 ml/4 tbsp olive oil, preferably Greek or Spanish
30 ml/2 tbsp garlic oil (see Introduction)
30 ml/2 tbsp lemon juice
salt and pepper
1 cos lettuce
50 g/2 oz chopped hazelnuts, toasted
1 medium open-textured loaf or 4 pitta breads, warmed

cos lettuce

hazelnuts

eggs

mint

olives

parsley

fennel

sun-dried tomatoes

spring onions (scallions)

1 Cover the bulghur wheat with boiling water and leave to soak for 15 minutes. Transfer to a metal sieve, position over a saucepan of boiling water, cover and steam for 10 minutes. Spread out on a metal tray and leave to cool.

COOK'S TIP
A popular way to eat tabbouleh is to shovel it into pockets of pitta bread. In Middle Eastern countries guests are invited to wrap tabbouleh in lettuce.

2 Hard-boil the eggs for 12 minutes. Cool under running water, shell and quarter. Halve and finely slice the fennel. Boil in salted water for 6 minutes, drain and cool under running water. Combine the eggs, fennel, spring onions, sun-dried tomatoes, parsley, mint and olives with the bulghur wheat. Dress with olive oil, garlic oil and lemon juice. Season well.

3 Wash the lettuce leaves and spin dry. Line an attractive salad bowl or plate with the leaves, pile in the tabbouleh and scatter with toasted hazelnuts. Serve with a basket of warm bread.

Goat's Cheese Salad with Buckwheat, Fresh Figs and Walnuts

The robust flavours of goat's cheese and buckwheat combine especially well with ripe figs and walnuts. The olive and nut oil dressing contains no vinegar and depends instead on the acidity of the cheese. Enjoy with a gutsy red wine from the Rhône or South of France.

Serves 4

INGREDIENTS
175 g/6 oz/¾ cup cous-cous
30 ml/2 tbsp toasted buckwheat
1 egg, hard-boiled
30 ml/2 tbsp chopped fresh parsley
60 ml/4 tbsp olive oil, preferably Sicilian
45 ml/3 tbsp walnut oil
125 g/4 oz rocket (arugula)
½ frisée lettuce
175 g/6 oz crumbly white goat's cheese
50 g/2 oz broken walnuts, toasted
4 ripe figs, trimmed and almost cut into four (leave the pieces joined at the base)

2 Shell the hard-boiled egg and pass it through a fine grater.

3 Toss the egg, parsley and cous-cous in a bowl. Combine the two oils and use half to moisten the cous-cous mixture.

1 Place the cous-cous and buckwheat in a bowl, cover with boiling water and leave to soak for 15 minutes. Place in a sieve if necessary to drain off any remaining water, then spread out on a metal tray and allow to cool.

4 Wash and spin the salad leaves, dress with the remaining oil and distribute between 4 large plates.

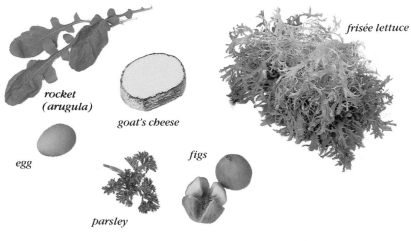

rocket (arugula)

goat's cheese

egg

parsley

figs

frisée lettuce

COOK'S TIP

Goats' cheeses vary in strength from the youngest, which are soft and mild, to strongly flavoured mature cheeses which have a firm and crumbly texture. Crumbly cheeses are best suited for salads.

5 Pile the cous-cous in the centre, crumble on the goat's cheese, scatter with toasted walnuts and add the figs.

Sweet Potato, Egg, Pork and Beetroot Salad

A delicious way to use up left-over roast pork. Sweet flavours balance well with the bitterness of the salad leaves.

Serves 4

INGREDIENTS
900 g/2 lb sweet potato, peeled and diced
salt
4 heads chicory
5 eggs, hard-boiled
450 g/1 lb pickled young beetroot
175 g/6 oz cold roast pork, sliced

DRESSING
75 ml/5 tbsp groundnut or sunflower oil
30 ml/2 tbsp white wine vinegar
10 ml/2 tsp Dijon mustard
5 ml/1 tsp fennel seeds, crushed

pork

sweet potato

eggs

beetroot

chicory

1 Bring the sweet potato to the boil in salted water and cook for 10–15 minutes or until soft. Drain and allow to cool.

2 To make the dressing, combine the oil, vinegar, mustard and fennel seeds in a screw-top jar and shake.

3 Separate the chicory leaves and arrange around the edge of 4 serving plates.

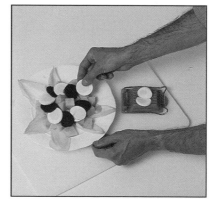

4 Dress the sweet potato and spoon over the salad leaves.

5 Shell the hard-boiled eggs. Slice the eggs and beetroot, and arrange to make an attractive border.

6 Cut the pork into 4 cm/1½ in fingers, moisten with dressing and pile into the centre. Season and serve.

Frankfurter Salad with Mustard and Caraway Dressing

A last-minute salad you can throw together using store-cupboard ingredients.

Serves 4

INGREDIENTS
700 g/1½ lb small new potatoes, scrubbed or scraped
2 eggs
350 g/12 oz frankfurters
1 butterhead or Batavian endive lettuce
225 g/8 oz young spinach, stems removed
salt and pepper

DRESSING
45 ml/3 tbsp safflower oil
30 ml/2 tbsp olive oil, preferably Spanish
15 ml/1 tbsp white wine vinegar
10 ml/2 tsp mustard
5 ml/1 tsp caraway seeds, crushed

1 Bring the potatoes to the boil in salted water and simmer for 20 minutes. Drain, cover and keep warm. Hard-boil the eggs for 12 minutes. Refresh in cold water, shell and cut into quarters.

2 Score the frankfurter skins cork-screw fashion with a small knife, then cover with boiling water and simmer for about 5 minutes to heat through. Drain well, cover and keep warm.

butterhead lettuce

eggs

frankfurters

spinach

new potatoes

3 Combine the dressing ingredients in a screw-top jar and shake.

4 Wash and spin the salad leaves, moisten with half of the dressing and distribute between 4 large plates.

5 Moisten the potatoes and frankfurters with the remainder of the dressing and scatter over the salad.

6 Finish with sections of hard-boiled egg, season and serve.

COOK'S TIP

Mustard has an important place in the salad maker's cupboard. Varieties differ from country to country and often suggest particular flavours. This salad has a German slant to it and calls for a sweet and sour German-style mustard. American mustards have a similar quality.

Pear and Pecan Nut Salad with Blue Cheese Dressing

Toasted pecan nuts have a special union with crisp white pears. Their robust flavours combine especially well with a rich blue cheese dressing and make this a salad to remember.

Serves 4

INGREDIENTS
75 g/3 oz/½ cup shelled pecan nuts, roughly chopped
3 crisp pears
175 g/6 oz young spinach, stems removed
1 escarole or butterhead lettuce
1 radicchio
30 ml/2 tbsp Blue Cheese and Chive Dressing
salt and pepper
crusty bread, to serve

1 Toast the pecan nuts under a moderate grill (broiler) to bring out their flavour.

2 Cut the pears into even slices, leaving the skin intact and discarding the cores.

3 Wash the salad leaves and spin dry. Add the pears together with the toasted pecans, then toss with the dressing. Distribute between 4 large plates and season with salt and pepper. Serve with warm crusty bread.

escarole

pears

pecan nuts

radicchio

spinach

Warm Fish Salad with Mango Dressing

This salad is best served during the summer months, preferably out of doors. The dressing combines the flavour of rich mango with hot chilli, ginger and lime.

Serves 4

INGREDIENTS
1 French loaf
4 redfish, black bream or porgy, each
    weighing about 275 g/10 oz
15 ml/1 tbsp vegetable oil
1 mango
1 cm/½ in fresh root ginger
1 fresh red chilli, seeded and finely
    chopped
30 ml/2 tbsp lime juice
30 ml/2 tbsp chopped fresh coriander
175 g/6 oz young spinach
150 g/5 oz pak choi
175 g/6 oz cherry tomatoes, halved

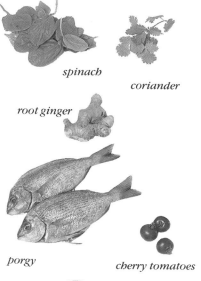

spinach

coriander

root ginger

porgy

cherry tomatoes

mango

1 Pre-heat the oven to 180°C/350°F/ Gas mark 4. Cut the French loaf into 20 cm/8 in lengths. Slice lengthways, then cut into thick fingers. Place the bread on a baking-sheet and dry in the oven for 15 minutes. Pre-heat the grill (broiler) or light the barbecue and allow the embers to settle. Slash the fish deeply on both sides and moisten with oil. Grill (broil) or barbecue for 6 minutes, turning once.

2 Place one half of the mango flesh in a food processor. Peel the ginger, grate finely, then add with the chilli, lime juice and coriander. Process until smooth. Adjust to a pouring consistency with 30–45 ml/2–3 tbsp water.

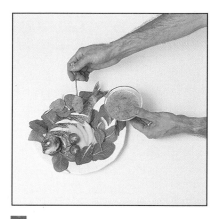

3 Wash the salad leaves and spin dry, then distribute them between 4 plates. Place the fish over the leaves. Spoon on the mango dressing and finish with slices of mango and tomato halves. Serve with fingers of crispy French bread.

COOK'S TIP

Other varieties of fish suitable for this salad include salmon, monkfish, tuna, sea bass and halibut.

Grilled Salmon and Spring Vegetable Salad

Spring is the time to enjoy sweet young vegetables. Cook them briefly, cool to room temperature, dress and serve with a piece of lightly grilled salmon topped with sorrel and quail's eggs.

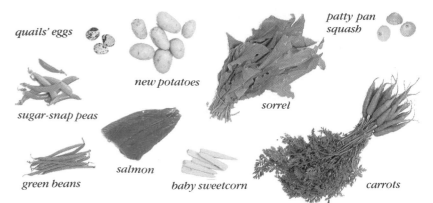

quails' eggs

new potatoes

sugar-snap peas

green beans

salmon

baby sweetcorn

patty pan squash

sorrel

carrots

Serves 4

INGREDIENTS
350 g/12 oz small new potatoes, scrubbed or scraped
4 quails' eggs
125 g/4 oz young carrots, peeled
125 g/4 oz baby sweetcorn
125 g/4 oz sugar-snap peas, topped and tailed
125 g/4 oz fine green beans, topped and tailed
125 g/4 oz young courgettes (zucchini)
125 g/4 oz patty pan squash (optional)

125 ml/4 fl oz French Dressing
4 salmon fillets, each weighing 150 g/5 oz, skinned
125 g/4 oz sorrel or young spinach, stems removed
salt and pepper

1 Bring the potatoes to the boil in salted water and cook for 15–20 minutes. Drain, cover and keep warm.

2 Cover the quails' eggs with boiling water and cook for 8 minutes. Refresh under cold water, shell and cut in half.

3 Bring a saucepan of salted water to the boil, add all the vegetables and cook for 2–3 minutes. Drain well. Place the hot vegetables and potatoes in a salad bowl, moisten with French Dressing and allow to cool.

4 Brush the salmon fillets with French Dressing and grill (broil) for 6 minutes, turning once.

5 Place the sorrel in a stainless-steel or enamel saucepan with 60 ml/4 tbsp French Dressing, cover and soften over a gentle heat for 2 minutes. Strain in a small sieve and cool to room temperature. Moisten the vegetables with the remaining dressing.

6 Divide the potatoes and vegetables between 4 large plates, then position a piece of salmon to one side of each plate. Finally place a spoonful of sorrel on each piece of salmon and top with a halved quail's egg. Season and serve at room temperature.

Salade Mouclade

Mouclade is a long-established dish from La Rochelle in south-west France. The dish consists of mussels in a light curry cream sauce and is usually served hot. Here the flavours appear in a salad of warm lentils and lightly cooked spinach. Serve at room temperature during the summer months.

Serves 4

INGREDIENTS

45 ml/3 tbsp olive oil, preferably
    French or Italian
1 medium onion, finely chopped
350 g/12 oz/1¾ cups Puy or green
    lentils, soaked for 2 hours
850 ml/1½ pints/3¾ cups
    vegetable stock
2 kg/4½ lb fresh mussels in their
    shells
75 ml/5 tbsp white wine
½ tsp mild curry paste
1 pinch saffron
30 ml/2 tbsp double (heavy) cream
salt and cayenne pepper
2 large carrots, peeled
4 stalks celery
900 g/2 lb young spinach, stems
    removed
15 ml/1 tbsp garlic oil (see
    Introduction)

carrot

onion

celery

green lentils   *mussels*

1 Heat the oil in a heavy saucepan and soften the onion for 6–8 minutes. Add the drained lentils and vegetable stock, bring to the boil and simmer for 45 minutes. Remove from the heat and cool.

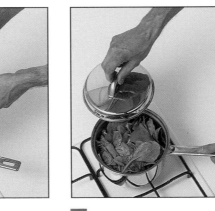

2 Clean the mussels thoroughly, discarding any that are damaged. Any that are open should close if given a sharp tap; if they fail to do so, discard these too. Place the mussels in a large saucepan, add the wine, cover and steam over a high heat for 12 minutes. Strain the mussels in a colander, collecting the cooking liquor in a bowl, and discard any that have not opened during the cooking. Allow the mussels to cool, then take them out of their shells.

3 Pass the mussel liquor through a fine sieve or muslin (cheesecloth) into a wide shallow saucepan to remove any grit or sand. Add the curry paste and saffron, then reduce over a high heat until almost dry. Remove from the heat, stir in the cream, season and combine with the mussels.

4 Bring a saucepan of salted water to the boil. Cut the carrot and celery into 5 cm/2 in matchsticks, cook for 3 minutes, drain, cool and moisten with olive oil.

5 Wash the spinach, put the wet leaves into a large saucepan, cover and steam for 30 seconds. Immerse in cold water and press the leaves dry with the back of a large spoon in a colander. Moisten with garlic oil, season and set aside.

6 Spoon the lentils into the centre of 4 large plates. Place 5 heaps of spinach around the edge of each one and position some carrot and celery on top of each heap. Spoon the mussels over the lentils and serve at room temperature.

Salade Niçoise

Salade Niçoise is a happy marriage of tuna fish, hard-boiled eggs, green beans and potatoes. Anchovies, olives and capers are often also included, but it is the first four ingredients that combine to make this a classic salad.

Serves 4

INGREDIENTS
700 g/1½ lb potatoes, peeled
salt and pepper
225 g/8 oz green beans, topped and
    tailed
3 eggs, hard-boiled
1 cos lettuce
125 ml/4 fl oz French Dressing
225 g/8 oz small plum tomatoes,
    quartered
400 g/14 oz canned tuna steak in oil,
    drained
25 g/1 oz canned anchovy fillets
30 ml/2 tbsp capers
12 black olives

1 Bring the potatoes to the boil in salted water and cook for 20 minutes. Boil the green beans for 6 minutes. Drain and cool the potatoes and beans under running water.

2 Slice the potatoes thickly. Shell and quarter the eggs.

3 Wash the lettuce and spin dry, then chop the leaves roughly. Moisten with half of the dressing in a large salad bowl.

cos lettuce

anchovy fillets

potatoes

green beans

olives

plum tomatoes

capers

4 Moisten the potatoes, green beans and tomatoes with dressing, then scatter over the salad leaves.

COOK'S TIP

The ingredients for Salade Niçoise can be prepared well in advance and should be assembled just before serving to retain flavour and freshness.

5 Break the tuna fish up with a fork and distribute over the salad with the anchovy fillets, capers and olives. Season to taste and serve.

Ratatouille

Ratatouille is a combination of tomatoes, onions, peppers, aubergines (eggplants) and courgettes (zucchini) cooked in olive oil and garlic. This Mediterranean dish is often served at room temperature during summer months and is delicious with a salad of white beans, a few anchovies and a basket of crispy bread.

Serves 4

INGREDIENTS
6 small aubergines (eggplants)
1 large Spanish onion, roughly chopped
3 cloves garlic, crushed
150 ml/5 fl oz/⅔ cup olive oil, preferably French or Spanish
225 g/8 oz courgettes (zucchini), thickly sliced
1 large green pepper, seeded and roughly chopped
350 g/12 oz ripe tomatoes, peeled and quartered
10 ml/2 tsp olive paste (optional)
30 ml/2 tbsp red wine vinegar
75 ml/5 tbsp chopped fresh herbs: parsley, basil, tarragon, oregano
salt and pepper

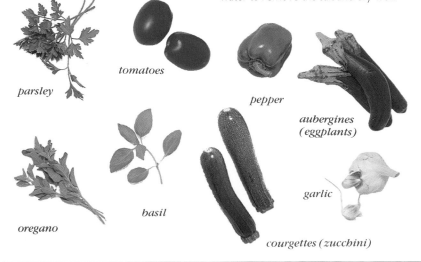

parsley

tomatoes

pepper

aubergines (eggplants)

oregano

basil

garlic

courgettes (zucchini)

2 Soften the onion and garlic in olive oil for 6–8 minutes. Add the aubergines, courgettes (zucchini), green pepper, tomatoes and olive paste (if using). Simmer uncovered for 40 minutes.

3 To finish, stir in the vinegar and herbs. Season to taste and allow to cool.

1 Halve the aubergines (eggplants), then slice thickly. If the aubergines are large, you will need to extract the bitter juices. To do this, sprinkle the cut surfaces generously with salt and secure between 2 large plates. After 20 minutes a clear liquid will emerge. Rinse well in cold water to remove the salt and dry well.

Waldorf Ham Salad

Waldorf salad first appeared at the Waldorf-Astoria Hotel, New York, in the 1890s. Originally it consisted of apples, celery and mayonnaise. It was commonly served with duck, ham and goose. This modern-day version often includes meat and is something of a meal in itself.

Serves 4

INGREDIENTS
3 apples, peeled
15 ml/1 tbsp lemon juice
2 slices cooked ham, each weighing
  175 g/6 oz
3 stalks celery
150 ml/5 fl oz/⅔ cup mayonnaise
1 escarole or Batavian endive lettuce
1 small radicchio, finely shredded
½ bunch watercress
45 ml/3 tbsp walnut oil or olive oil
50 g/2 oz/½ cup broken walnuts,
  toasted
salt and pepper

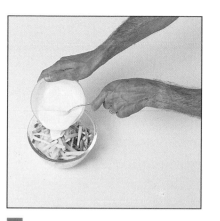

2 Add the mayonnaise to the apples, ham and celery and mix well.

3 Wash and spin the salad leaves. Shred the leaves finely, then moisten with walnut oil. Distribute the leaves beteen 4 plates. Pile the mayonnaise mixture in the centre, scatter with toasted walnuts, season and serve.

1 Core, slice and shred the apples finely. Moisten with lemon juice to keep them white. Cut the ham into 5 cm/2 in strips, then cut the celery into similar-sized pieces, and combine in a bowl.

apple

celery

watercress

walnuts

radicchio

escarole lettuce

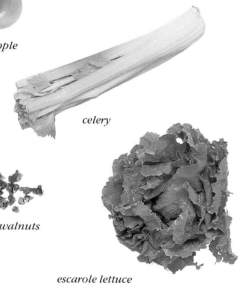

Caesar Salad

There are many stories about the origin of Caesar Salad. The most likely is that it was invented by an Italian, Caesar Cardini, who owned a restaurant in Mexico in the 1920s. Simplicity is the key to its success.

Serves 4

INGREDIENTS
3 slices day-old bread, 1 cm/½ in thick
60 ml/4 tbsp garlic oil (see Introduction)
salt and pepper
50 g/2 oz piece Parmesan cheese
1 cos lettuce

DRESSING
2 egg yolks, as fresh as possible
25 g/1 oz canned anchovy fillets, roughly chopped
½ tsp French mustard
125 ml/4 fl oz/½ cup olive oil, preferably Italian
15 ml/1 tbsp white wine vinegar

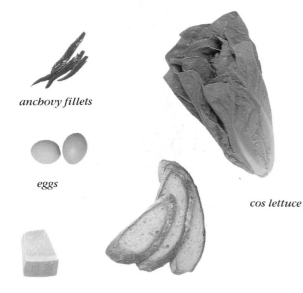

anchovy fillets

eggs

cos lettuce

Parmesan cheese　　*bread*

COOK'S TIP
The classic dressing for Caesar Salad is made with raw egg yolks. Ensure you use only the freshest eggs, bought from a reputable dealer. Expectant mothers, young children and the elderly are not advised to eat raw egg yolks. You could omit them from the dressing and grate hard-boiled yolks on top of the salad instead.

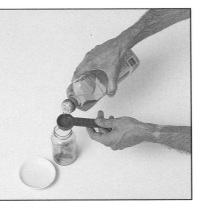

1 To make the dressing, combine the egg yolks, anchovies, mustard, oil and vinegar in a screw-top jar and shake well.

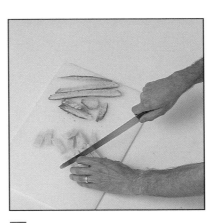

2 Remove the crusts from the bread with a serrated knife and cut into 2.5 cm/1 in fingers.

3 Heat the garlic oil in a large frying-pan (skillet), add the pieces of bread and fry until golden. Sprinkle with salt and leave to drain on absorbent kitchen paper (paper towels).

4 Cut thin shavings from the Parmesan cheese with a vegetable peeler.

5 Wash the salad leaves and spin dry. Smother with the dressing, and scatter with garlic croûtons and Parmesan cheese. Season and serve.

Gado Gado

Gado Gado is a traditional Indonesian salad around which friends and family gather to eat. Fillings are chosen and wrapped in a lettuce leaf. The parcel is then dipped in a spicy peanut sauce and eaten, usually with the left hand. Salad ingredients vary according to what is in season.

Serves 4

INGREDIENTS
2 medium potatoes, peeled
salt
3 eggs
175 g/6 oz green beans, topped and tailed
1 cos lettuce
4 tomatoes, cut into wedges
125 g/4 oz bean sprouts
½ cucumber, peeled and cut into fingers
150 g/5 oz giant white radish (mooli), peeled and grated
175 g/6 oz bean curd (tofu), cut into large dice
350 g/12 oz large cooked peeled prawns (shrimp)
1 small bunch fresh coriander

SPICY PEANUT SAUCE
150 g/5 oz/½ cup smooth peanut butter
juice of ½ lemon
2 shallots or 1 small onion, finely chopped
1 clove garlic, crushed
1–2 small fresh red chillies, seeded and finely chopped
30 ml/2 tbsp South-east Asian fish sauce (optional)
150 ml/5 fl oz/⅔ cup coconut milk, canned or fresh
15 ml/1 tbsp caster (superfine) sugar

1 To make the Spicy Peanut Sauce, combine the ingredients in a food processor until smooth.

coriander

potatoes

prawns (shrimp)

cos lettuce

green beans

cucumber

eggs

bean sprouts

giant white radish (mooli)

2 Bring the potatoes to the boil in salted water and simmer for 20 minutes. Bring a second pan of salted water to the boil. To save using too many pans, cook the eggs and beans together: lower the eggs into the boiling water in the second pan; then, after 6 minutes, add the beans and boil for a further 6 minutes. (Hard-boiled eggs should have a total of 12 minutes.) Cool the potatoes, eggs and beans under running water.

3 Wash and spin the salad leaves and use the outer leaves to line a large platter. Pile the remainder to one side of the platter.

4 Slice the potatoes. Shell and quarter the eggs. Arrange the potatoes, eggs, beans and tomatoes in separate piles. Arrange the other salad ingredients in a similar way to cover the platter.

HANDLING CHILLIES

Red chillies are considered to be sweeter and hotter than green ones. Smaller varieties of both red and green are likely to be more pungent than large varieties. You can lessen the intensity of a fresh chilli by splitting it open and removing the white seed-bearing membrane. The residue given off when chillies are cut can cause serious burns to the skin. Be sure to wash your hands thoroughly after handling raw chillies and avoid touching your eyes or any sensitive skin areas.

5 Turn the Spicy Peanut Sauce into an attractive bowl and bring to the table with the salad.

Poor Boy Steak Salad

'Poor Boy' started life in the Italian Creole community of New Orleans when the poor survived on sandwiches filled with left-over scraps. Times have improved since then, and today the 'Poor Boy' sandwich is commonly filled with tender beef steak and other goodies. This is a salad version of 'Poor Boy'.

Serves 4

INGREDIENTS
4 sirloin or rump steaks, each
  weighing 175 g/6 oz
1 escarole lettuce
1 bunch watercress
4 tomatoes, quartered
4 large gherkins (dill pickles), sliced
4 spring onions (scallions), sliced
4 canned artichoke hearts, halved
175 g/6 oz button mushrooms, sliced
12 green olives
125 ml/4 fl oz French Dressing
salt and black pepper

1 Season the steaks with black pepper. Cook the steaks under a moderate grill (broiler) for 6–8 minutes, turning once, until medium-rare. Cover and leave to rest in a warm place.

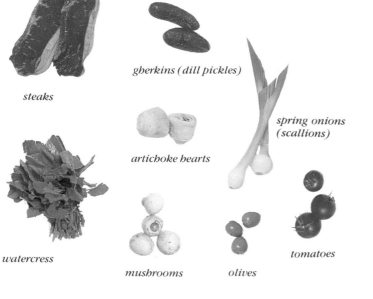

steaks

gherkins (dill pickles)

artichoke hearts

spring onions (scallions)

watercress

mushrooms

olives

tomatoes

2 Wash the salad leaves and spin dry. Combine with the remainder of the ingredients (except the steak) and toss with the French Dressing.

3 Divide the salad between 4 plates. Slice each steak diagonally and position over the salad. Season with salt and serve.

Russian Salad

Russian salad became fashionable in the hotel dining rooms of the 1920s and 1930s. Originally it consisted of lightly cooked vegetables, egg, shellfish and mayonnaise. Today we find it diced in plastic pots in supermarkets. This version recalls better days and plays on the theme of the Fabergé egg.

Serves 4

INGREDIENTS
125 g/4 oz large button mushrooms
125 ml/4 fl oz/½ cup mayonnaise
15 ml/1 tbsp lemon juice
350 g/12 oz cooked peeled prawns (shrimp)
1 large gherkin (dill pickle), chopped, or 30 ml/2 tbsp capers
125 g/4 oz broad beans
125 g/4 oz small new potatoes, scrubbed or scraped
125 g/4 oz young carrots, trimmed and peeled
125 g/4 oz baby sweetcorn
125 g/4 oz baby turnips, trimmed
15 ml/1 tbsp olive oil, preferably French or Italian
4 eggs, hard-boiled and shelled
25 g/1 oz canned anchovy fillets, cut into fine strips
salt, pepper and paprika

2 Bring a large saucepan of salted water to the boil, add the broad beans and cook for 3 minutes. Drain and cool under running water, then pinch the beans between thumb and forefinger to release them from their tough skins. Boil the potatoes for 20 minutes and the remaining vegetables for 6 minutes. Drain and cool under running water.

3 Moisten the vegetables with oil and divide between 4 shallow bowls. Spoon on the dressed prawns and place a hard-boiled egg in the centre. Decorate the egg with strips of anchovy and sprinkle with paprika.

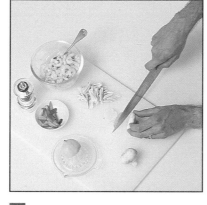

1 Slice the mushrooms thinly, then cut into matchsticks. Combine the mayonnaise and lemon juice. Fold half of the mayonnaise into the mushrooms and prawns (shrimp), add the chopped gherkin (dill pickle), then season to taste.

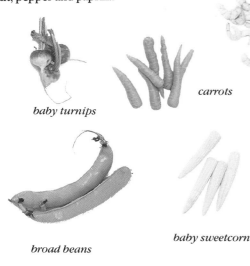

prawns (shrimp)

carrots

baby turnips

new potatoes

broad beans

baby sweetcorn

mushrooms

San Francisco Salad

California is a salad maker's paradise and is renowned for the healthiness of its produce. San Francisco has become the salad capital of California, although this recipe is based on a salad served at the Chez Panisse restaurant in Berkeley.

Serves 4

INGREDIENTS

900 g/2 lb langoustines, Dublin Bay
   prawns or Danish lobster
salt and cayenne pepper
50 g/2 oz bulb fennel, sliced
2 ripe medium tomatoes, quartered,
   and 4 small tomatoes
30 ml/2 tbsp olive oil, plus extra for
   moistening the salad leaves
60 ml/4 tbsp brandy
150 ml/5 fl oz/⅔ cup dry white wine
200 ml/7 fl oz can lobster or crab
   bisque
30 ml/2 tbsp chopped fresh tarragon
45 ml/3 tbsp double (heavy) cream
225 g/8 oz green beans, topped and
   tailed
2 oranges
175 g/6 oz lamb's lettuce
125 g/4 oz rocket (arugula)
½ frisée lettuce

frisée lettuce

    langoustines

tomatoes   *fennel*   *orange*

lamb's lettuce

rocket (arugula)

1 Bring a large saucepan of salted water to the boil, add the langoustines and simmer for 10 minutes. Refresh under cold running water.

2 Pre-heat the oven to 220°C/425°F/ Gas mark 7. Twist the tails from all but 4 of the langoustines: reserve these to garnish the dish. Peel the outer shell from the tail meat. Put the tail peelings, carapace and claws in a roasting-tray (roasting-pan) with the fennel and tomatoes. Toss with 30 ml/2 tbsp oil and roast near the top of the oven for 20 minutes to bring out the flavours.

3 Remove the roasting-tray from the oven and place it over a moderate heat on top of the stove. Add the brandy and ignite to release the flavour of the alcohol. Add the wine and simmer briefly.

4 Transfer the contents of the roasting-tray to a food processor and reduce to a coarse purée: this will take only 10–15 seconds. Rub the purée through a fine nylon sieve into a bowl. Add the lobster bisque, tarragon and cream. Season to taste with salt and a little cayenne pepper.

5 Bring a saucepan of salted water to the boil and cook the beans for 6 minutes. Drain and cool under running water. To segment the oranges, cut the peel from the top and bottom, and then from the sides, with a serrated knife. Loosen the segments by cutting between the membranes and the flesh.

6 Wash and spin the salad leaves. Moisten with olive oil and distribute between 4 serving plates. Fold the langoustine tails into the dressing and distribute between the plates. Add the beans, orange segments and small tomatoes, decorate each plate with a whole langoustine and serve warm.

Prawn Salad with Curry Dressing

Curry spices add an unexpected twist to this salad. Warm flavours combine especially well with sweet prawns and grated apple.

Serves 4

INGREDIENTS
1 ripe tomato
½ iceberg lettuce, shredded
1 small onion
1 small bunch fresh coriander
15 ml/1 tbsp lemon juice
salt
450 g/1 lb cooked peeled prawns (shrimp)
1 apple, peeled

DRESSING
75 ml/5 tbsp mayonnaise
5 ml/1 tsp mild curry paste
15 ml/1 tbsp tomato ketchup

TO DECORATE
8 whole prawns
8 lemon wedges
4 sprigs fresh coriander

prawns (shrimp)
coriander
tomato
apple
lemon
onion

1 To peel the tomato, pierce the skin with a knife and immerse in boiling water for 20 seconds. Drain and cool under running water. Peel off the skin. Halve the tomato, push the seeds out with your thumb and discard them. Cut the flesh into large dice.

2 Finely shred the lettuce, onion and coriander. Add the tomato, moisten with lemon juice and season with salt.

3 To make the dressing, combine the mayonnaise, curry paste and tomato ketchup in a small bowl. Add 30 ml/2 tbsp water to thin the dressing and season to taste with salt.

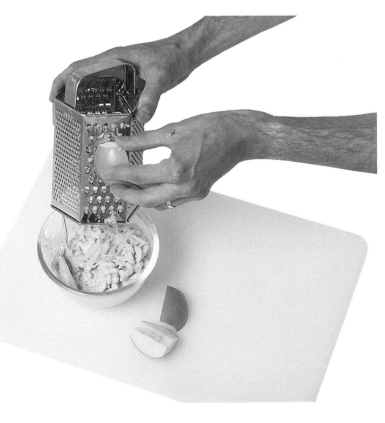

4 Combine the prawns (shrimp) with the dressing. Quarter and core the apple and grate into the mixture.

COOK'S TIP

Fresh coriander is inclined to wilt if kept out of water. Keep it in a jar of water in the refrigerator covered with a plastic bag and it will stay fresh for several days.

5 Distribute the shredded lettuce mixture between 4 plates or bowls. Pile the prawn mixture in the centre of each and decorate with 2 whole prawns, 2 lemon wedges and a sprig of coriander.

Apple Coleslaw

The term coleslaw stems from the Dutch *koolsla*, meaning 'cool cabbage'. There are many variations of this salad; this recipe combines the sweet flavours of apple and carrot with celery salt. Coleslaw is traditionally served with cold ham.

Serves 4

INGREDIENTS
450 g/1 lb white cabbage
1 medium onion
2 apples, peeled and cored
175 g/6 oz carrots, peeled
150 ml/5 fl oz/⅔ cup mayonnaise
5 ml/1 tsp celery salt
black pepper

carrots

onion

apple

white cabbage

1 Discard the outside leaves of the cabbage if they are dirty, cut the cabbage into 5 cm/2 in wedges, then remove the stem section.

2 Feed the cabbage and the onion through a food processor fitted with a slicing blade. Change to a grating blade and grate the apples and carrots. Alternatively use a hand grater and vegetable slicer.

3 Combine the salad ingredients in a large bowl. Fold in the mayonnaise and season with celery salt and freshly ground black pepper.

COOK'S TIP

This recipe can be adapted easily to suit different tastes. You could add 125 g/4 oz/½ cup chopped walnuts or raisins for added texture. For a richer coleslaw, add 125 g/4 oz/½ cup grated Cheddar cheese. You may find you will need smaller portions, as the cheese makes a more filling dish.

Potato Salad with Egg and Lemon Dressing

Potato salads are a popular addition to any salad spread and are enjoyed with an assortment of cold meats and fish. This recipe draws on the contrasting flavours of egg and lemon. Chopped parsley provides a fresh finish.

Serves 4

INGREDIENTS
900 g/2 lb new potatoes, scrubbed or scraped
salt and pepper
1 medium onion, finely chopped
1 egg, hard-boiled
300 ml/10 fl oz/1¼ cups mayonnaise
1 clove garlic, crushed
finely grated zest and juice of 1 lemon
60 ml/4 tbsp chopped fresh parsley

COOK'S TIP
At certain times of the year potatoes are inclined to fall apart when boiled. This usually coincides with the end of a particular season when potatoes become starchy. Early-season varieties are therefore best for making salads.

egg

garlic

onion

lemon

new potatoes

1 Bring the potatoes to the boil in a saucepan of salted water. Simmer for 20 minutes. Drain and allow to cool. Cut the potatoes into large dice, season well and combine with the onion.

2 Shell the hard-boiled egg and grate into a mixing bowl, then add the mayonnaise. Combine the garlic and lemon zest and juice in a small bowl and stir into the mayonnaise.

3 Fold in the chopped parsley, mix thoroughly into the potatoes and serve.

Sweet Turnip Salad with Horseradish and Caraway

The robust-flavoured turnip partners well with the taste of horseradish and caraway seeds. This salad is delicious with cold roast beef or smoked trout.

Serves 4

INGREDIENTS
350 g/12 oz medium turnips
2 spring onions (scallions), white part only, chopped
15 ml/1 tbsp caster (superfine) sugar
salt
30 ml/2 tbsp horseradish cream
10 ml/2 tsp caraway seeds

turnips

spring onions (scallions)

COOK'S TIP
If turnips are not available, giant white radish (mooli) can be used as a substitute.

1 Peel, slice and shred the turnips – or grate them if you wish.

2 Add the spring onions (scallions), sugar and salt, then rub together with your hands to soften the turnip.

3 Fold in the horseradish cream and caraway seeds.

Tomato and Feta Cheese Salad

Sweet sun-ripened tomatoes are rarely more delicious than when served with feta cheese and olive oil. This salad, popular in Greece and Turkey, is enjoyed as a light meal with pieces of crispy bread.

Serves 4

INGREDIENTS
900 g/2 lb tomatoes
200 g/7 oz feta cheese
125 ml/4 fl oz/½ cup olive oil,
  preferably Greek
12 black olives
4 sprigs fresh basil
black pepper

COOK'S TIP

Feta cheese has a strong flavour and can be salty. The least salty variety is imported from Greece and Turkey, and is available from specialist delicatessens.

2 Slice the tomatoes thickly and arrange in a shallow dish.

3 Crumble the cheese over the tomatoes, sprinkle with olive oil, then strew with olives and fresh basil. Season with freshly ground black pepper and serve at room temperature.

1 Remove the tough cores from the tomatoes with a small knife.

tomatoes

basil

feta cheese

olives

Soft Leeks with Parsley, Egg and Walnut Dressing

In French cooking leeks are valued for their smooth texture as well as for their flavour. Here they are served as a *salade tiède* (warm salad), with an earthy-rich sauce of parsley, egg and walnut. Serve as a side salad with plainly grilled (broiled) or poached fish and new potatoes.

Serves 4

INGREDIENTS
700 g/1½ lb young leeks
1 egg

DRESSING
25 g/1 oz fresh parsley
30 ml/2 tbsp olive oil, preferably
    French
juice of ½ lemon
50 g/2 oz/½ cup broken walnuts,
    toasted
5 ml/1 tsp caster (superfine) sugar
salt and pepper

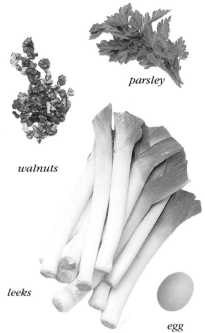

parsley

walnuts

leeks

egg

1 Bring a saucepan of salted water to the boil. Cut the leeks into 10 cm/4 in lengths and rinse well to flush out any grit or soil. Cook the leeks for 8 minutes. Drain and part-cool under running water.

2 Lower the egg into boiling water and cook for 12 minutes. Cool under running water, shell and set aside.

3 For the dressing, finely chop the parsley in a food processor.

4 Add the olive oil, lemon juice and toasted walnuts. Blend for 1–2 minutes until smooth.

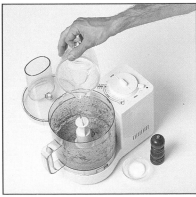

5 Adjust the consistency with about 90 ml/6 tbsp/⅓ cup water. Add the sugar and season to taste with salt and pepper.

6 Place the leeks on an attractive plate, then spoon on the sauce. Finely grate the hard-boiled egg and scatter over the sauce. Serve at room temperature.

Tzatziki

Tzatziki is a Greek cucumber salad dressed with yogurt, mint and garlic. It is typically served with grilled lamb and chicken, but is also good with salmon and trout.

Serves 4

INGREDIENTS
1 cucumber
5 ml/1 tsp salt
45 ml/3 tbsp finely chopped fresh
    mint, plus a few sprigs to garnish
1 clove garlic, crushed
5 ml/1 tsp caster (superfine) sugar
200m ml/7 fl oz strained Greek-style
    (plain) yogurt
paprika, to garnish (optional)

mint

cucumber

1 Peel the cucumber. Reserve a little to use as a garnish if you wish and cut the rest in half lengthways. Remove the seeds with a teaspoon and discard. Slice the cucumber thinly and combine with salt. Leave for approximately 15–20 minutes. Salt will soften the cucumber and draw out any bitter juices.

2 Combine the mint, garlic, sugar and yogurt in a bowl, reserving a few sprigs of mint as decoration.

3 Rinse the cucumber in a sieve under cold running water to flush away the salt. Drain well and combine with the yogurt. Decorate with cucumber and mint. Serve cold. Tzatziki is traditionally garnished with paprika.

COOK'S TIP

If preparing Tzatziki in a hurry, leave out the method for salting cucumber at the end of step 1. The cucumber will have a more crunchy texture, and will be slightly less sweet.

Green Bean Salad with Egg Topping

When green beans are fresh and plentiful, serve them lightly cooked as a salad starter topped with butter-fried breadcrumbs, egg and parsley.

Serves 4

INGREDIENTS
700 g/1½ lb green beans, topped and
    tailed
salt
30 ml/2 tbsp garlic oil (see
    Introduction)
30 ml/2 tbsp butter
50 g/2 oz/1 cup fresh white
    breadcrumbs
60 ml/4 tbsp chopped fresh parsley
1 egg, hard-boiled and shelled

parsley

egg

green beans

2 Heat the butter in a large frying-pan (skillet), add the breadcrumbs and fry until golden. Remove from the heat, add the parsley, then grate in the hard-boiled egg.

3 Place the beans in a shallow serving dish and spoon on the breadcrumb topping. Serve at room temperature.

1 Bring a large saucepan of salted water to the boil. Add the beans and cook for 6 minutes. Drain well, toss in garlic oil and allow to cool.

COOK'S TIP

Few cooks need reminding how to boil an egg, but many are faced with the problem of a dark ring around the yolk when cooked. This is caused by boiling for longer than the optimum period of 12 minutes. Allow boiled eggs to cool in water for easy peeling.

White Bean and Celery Salad

This simple bean salad is a delicious alternative to the potato salad that seems to appear on every salad menu. If you do not have time to soak and cook dried beans, use canned ones.

Serves 4

INGREDIENTS
450 g/1 lb dried white beans (haricot, canellini, navy or butter beans) or 3 × 400 g/14 oz cans white beans
1 litre/1¾ pints/4½ cups vegetable stock, made from a cube
3 stalks celery, cut into 1 cm/½ in strips
125 ml/4 fl oz French Dressing
45 ml/3 tbsp chopped fresh parsley
salt and pepper

parsley

white beans

celery

1 If using dried beans, cover with plenty of cold water and soak for at least 4 hours. Discard the soaking water, then place the beans in a heavy saucepan. Cover with fresh water, bring to the boil and simmer without a lid for 1½ hours, or until the skins are broken. Cooked beans will squash readily between a thumb and forefinger. Drain the beans. If using canned beans, drain, rinse and use from this stage in the recipe.

2 Place the cooked beans in a large saucepan. Add the vegetable stock and celery, bring to the boil, cover and simmer for 15 minutes. Drain thoroughly. Moisten the beans with the dressing and leave to cool.

3 Add the chopped parsley and season to taste with salt and pepper.

COOK'S TIP

Dried beans that have been kept for longer than 6 months will need soaking overnight to lessen their cooking time. As a rule, the less time beans have been kept in store, the shorter the soaking and cooking time they need. The times given here are suited to freshly purchased beans.

Guacamole Salad Dip

Creamy rich guacamole is a welcome sight at any party gathering. If you are cooking a Mexican meal, serve it as a salad dip with tortilla chips, raw vegetables and crispy potato skins.

Serves 4

INGREDIENTS
2 large ripe avocados
2 cloves garlic, crushed
1 small onion, finely chopped
60 ml/4 tbsp lemon juice
1 fresh green chilli, seeded and
    chopped (optional)
45 ml/3 tbsp chopped fresh coriander
salt
Tabasco sauce

TO SERVE
5 large potatoes
15 ml/1 tbsp vegetable oil
4 stalks celery, cut into fingers
3 large ripe tomatoes, cut into wedges
1 mild Spanish onion, cut into strips
tortilla chips
8 Jalapeno or soft green chillies
    (optional)

1 Halve each avocado lengthways, discard the stone and scoop the flesh into a food processor.

COOK'S TIP

Choose avocados that yield to firm pressure near the stem. The fruits ripen most effectively if they are kept in a brown paper bag with ripe bananas or mangoes.

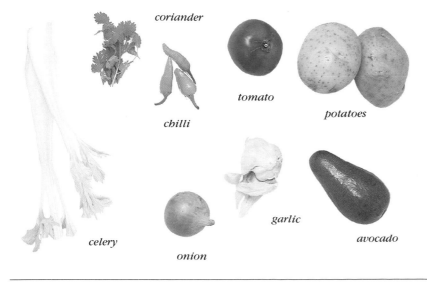

coriander

chilli

tomato

potatoes

celery

onion

garlic

avocado

2 Add the garlic, onion, lemon juice and green chilli (if using). Blend roughly. Add the coriander and season to taste with salt and Tabasco sauce. Cover closely with cling film (plastic wrap) to prevent discolouration.

3 To prepare potato skins, thickly peel the potatoes: you should aim for 6–8 large pieces of peel from each one. Cover with boiling water and cook for 5 minutes. Meanwhile pre-heat the grill (broiler) or barbecue to a moderate temperature. Drain the potato skins well, toss in oil, season with salt and grill (broil) until crisp. Turn the guacamole out into an attractive bowl, place on a serving plate with the dipping ingredients and serve.

Rocket, Pear and Parmesan Salad

For a sophisticated start to an elaborate meal, try this simple salad of honey-rich pears, fresh Parmesan and aromatic leaves of rocket (arugula). Enjoy with a young Beaujolais or chilled Lambrusco wine.

Serves 4

INGREDIENTS
3 ripe pears, Williams or Packhams
10 ml/2 tsp lemon juice
45 ml/3 tbsp hazelnut or walnut oil
125 g/4 oz rocket (arugula)
75 g/3 oz Parmesan cheese
black pepper
open-textured bread, to serve

rocket (arugula)

Parmesan cheese

pears

1 Peel and core the pears and slice thickly. Moisten with lemon juice to keep the flesh white.

2 Combine the nut oil with the pears. Add the rocket leaves and toss.

3 Turn the salad out on to 4 small plates and top with shavings of Parmesan cheese. Season with freshly ground black pepper and serve.

COOK'S TIP
If you are unable to buy rocket easily, you can grow your own from early spring to late summer.

Cachumbar

Cachumbar is a salad relish most commonly served with Indian curries. There are many versions, although this one will leave your mouth feeling cool and fresh after a spicy meal.

Serves 4

INGREDIENTS
3 ripe tomatoes
2 spring onions (scallions), chopped
¼ tsp caster (superfine) sugar
salt
45 ml/3 tbsp chopped fresh coriander

tomatoes

coriander

spring onion (scallion)

COOK'S TIP
Cachumbar also makes a fine accompaniment to fresh crab, lobster and shellfish.

2 Halve the tomatoes, remove the seeds and dice the flesh.

3 Combine the tomatoes with the spring onions, sugar, salt and chopped coriander. Serve at room temperature.

1 Remove the tough cores from the tomatoes with a small knife.

Thai Scented Fish Salad

For a tropical taste of the Far East, try this delicious fish salad scented with coconut, fruit and warm Thai spices.

Serves 4

INGREDIENTS
350 g/12 oz fillet of red mullet, sea
   bream or snapper
1 cos lettuce
½ lollo biondo lettuce
1 papaya or mango, peeled and sliced
1 pithaya, peeled and sliced
1 large ripe tomato, cut into wedges
½ cucumber, peeled and cut into
   batons
3 spring onions (scallions), sliced

MARINADE
5 ml/1 tsp coriander seeds
5 ml/1 tsp fennel seeds
½ tsp cumin seeds
5 ml/1 tsp caster (superfine) sugar
½ tsp hot chilli sauce
30 ml/2 tbsp garlic oil (see
   Introduction)
salt

DRESSING
15 ml/1 tbsp creamed coconut
salt
60 ml/4 tbsp groundnut or safflower
   oil
finely grated zest and juice of 1 lime
1 fresh red chilli, seeded and finely
   chopped
5 ml/1 tsp sugar
45 ml/ 3 tbsp chopped fresh coriander

lollo biondo lettuce   *cucumber*

tomato

red mullet

spring onions (scallions)

cos lettuce

papaya

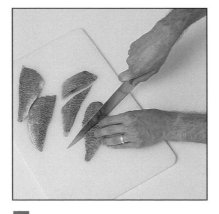

1 Cut the fish into even strips and place on a plate or in a shallow bowl.

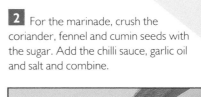

2 For the marinade, crush the coriander, fennel and cumin seeds with the sugar. Add the chilli sauce, garlic oil and salt and combine.

3 Spread the marinade over the fish, cover and leave to stand in a cool place for at least 20 minutes – longer if you have time.

4 To make the dressing, place the creamed coconut and salt in a screw-top jar with 45 ml/3 tbsp boiling water and allow to dissolve. Add the oil, lime zest and juice, red chilli, sugar and chopped fresh coriander. Shake well and set aside.

5 Wash and spin the lettuce leaves. Combine with the papaya, pithaya, tomato, cucumber and spring onions (scallions). Toss with the dressing, then distribute between 4 large plates.

6 Heat a large non-stick frying-pan (skillet), add the fish and cook for 5 minutes, turning once. Place the cooked fish over the salad and serve.

COOK'S TIP

If planning ahead, you can leave the fish in its marinade for up to 8 hours. The dressing can also be made in advance minus the fresh coriander. Store at room temperature and add the coriander when you are ready to assemble the salad.

Melon and Parma Ham Salad with Strawberry Salsa

Sections of cool fragrant melon wrapped with slices of air-dried ham make a delicious salad starter. If strawberries are in season, serve with a savoury-sweet strawberry salsa and watch it disappear.

Serves 4

INGREDIENTS
1 large melon, cantaloupe, galia or charentais
175 g/6 oz Parma or Serrano ham, thinly sliced

SALSA
225 g/8 oz strawberries
5 ml/1 tsp caster (superfine) sugar
30 ml/2 tbsp groundnut or sunflower oil
15 ml/1 tbsp orange juice
½ tsp finely grated orange zest
½ tsp finely grated fresh root ginger
salt and black pepper

2 To make the salsa, hull the strawberries and cut them into large dice. Place in a small mixing bowl with the sugar and crush lightly to release the juices. Add the oil, orange juice, zest and ginger. Season with salt and a generous twist of black pepper.

3 Arrange the melon on a serving plate, lay the ham over the top and serve with a bowl of salsa.

1 Halve the melon and take the seeds out with a spoon. Cut the rind away with a paring knife, then slice the melon thickly. Chill until ready to serve.

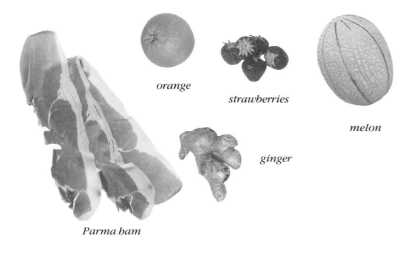

orange

strawberries

ginger

melon

Parma ham

Wild Mushroom Salad with Parma Ham

Autumn provides a wealth of new flavours for the salad maker. Most treasured of all are wild mushrooms found mainly in deciduous woodland. If you are not familiar with edible species, larger supermarkets and specialist delicatessens often sell a range of wild and cultivated mushrooms.

Serves 4

INGREDIENTS

175 g/6 oz Parma ham, thickly sliced
45 ml/3 tbsp butter
450 g/1 lb wild and cultivated
    mushrooms (chanterelles, field
    blewits, oyster mushrooms,
    champignons de Paris), sliced
60 ml/4 tbsp brandy
½ oakleaf lettuce
½ frisée lettuce
15 ml/1 tbsp walnut oil

HERB PANCAKES

45 ml/3 tbsp plain (all-purpose) flour
75 ml/5 tbsp milk
1 egg plus 1 egg yolk
60 ml/4 tbsp freshly grated Parmesan
    cheese
45 ml/3 tbsp chopped fresh herbs:
    parsley, thyme, tarragon, marjoram,
    chives
salt and black pepper

frisée lettuce

mushrooms

Parma ham

1 To make the pancakes, combine the flour with the milk in a measuring jug. Beat in the egg and egg yolk with the cheese, herbs and seasoning. Place a non-stick frying-pan (skillet) over a steady heat. Pour in enough mixture to coat the bottom of the pan.

2 When the batter has set, turn the pancake over and cook briefly on the other side. Turn out and cool.

3 Roll the pancakes together and cut into 1 cm/½ in ribbons. Cut the ham into similar-sized ribbons and toss together with the pancake ribbons.

4 Heat the butter in a frying-pan until it begins to brown. Add the mushrooms and cook for 6–8 minutes. Add the brandy and ignite with a match. The flames will subside when the alcohol has burnt off. Wash and spin the salad leaves, moisten with walnut oil and distribute between 4 plates. Place the ham and pancake ribbons in the centre, spoon on the mushrooms, season and serve warm.

Rockburger Salad with Sesame Croûtons

This salad plays on the ingredients that make up the all-American beefburger in a sesame bun. Inside the burger is a special layer of Roquefort, a blue ewe's-milk cheese from France.

Serves 4

INGREDIENTS
900 g/2 lb lean minced (ground) beef
1 egg
1 medium onion, finely chopped
10 ml/2 tsp French mustard
½ tsp celery salt
black pepper
125 g/4 oz Roquefort or other blue
  cheese
1 large sesame seed loaf
45 ml/3 tbsp olive oil, preferably
  Spanish
1 small iceberg lettuce
50 g/2 oz rocket (arugula)
  or watercress
125 ml/4 fl oz French Dressing
4 ripe tomatoes, quartered
4 large spring onions (scallions),
  sliced

iceberg lettuce

rocket (arugula)

egg

minced (ground) beef

blue cheese

sesame seed loaf

COOK'S TIP
If you're planning ahead, it's a good idea to freeze the filled burgers between pieces of waxed paper. They will keep in the freezer for up to 8 weeks.

1 Place the minced (ground) beef, egg, onion, mustard, celery salt and pepper in a mixing bowl. Combine thoroughly. Divide the mixture into 16 portions, each weighing 50 g/2 oz.

2 Flatten the pieces between 2 sheets of polythene or waxed paper to form 13 cm/5 in rounds.

3 Place 15 g/½ oz of the cheese on 8 of the thin burgers. Sandwich with the remainder and press the edges firmly. Store between pieces of polythene (plastic wrap) or waxed paper and chill until ready to cook.

4 To make the sesame croûtons, pre-heat the grill (broiler) to a moderate temperature. Remove the sesame crust from the bread, then cut the crust into short fingers. Moisten with olive oil and toast evenly for 10–15 minutes.

5 Season the burgers and grill (broil) for 10 minutes, turning once.

6 Wash the salad leaves and spin dry. Toss with the dressing, then distribute between 4 large plates. Place 2 rockburgers in the centre of each plate and the tomatoes, spring onions (scallions) and sesame croûtons around the edge.

Grilled Chicken Salad with Lavender and Sweet Herbs

Lavender may seem like an odd salad ingredient, but its delightful scent has a natural affinity with sweet garlic, orange and other wild herbs. A serving of corn meal polenta makes this salad both filling and delicious.

Serves 4

INGREDIENTS
4 boneless chicken breasts
850 ml/1½ pints/3¾ cups light chicken stock
175 g/6 oz/1 cup fine polenta or corn meal
50 g/2 oz butter
450 g/1 lb young spinach
175 g/6 oz lamb's lettuce
8 sprigs fresh lavender
8 small tomatoes, halved
salt and black pepper

LAVENDER MARINADE
6 fresh lavender flowers
10 ml/2 tsp finely grated orange zest
2 cloves garlic, crushed
10 ml/2 tsp clear honey
salt
30 ml/2 tbsp olive oil, French or Italian
10 ml/2 tsp chopped fresh thyme
10 ml/2 tsp chopped fresh marjoram

lavender   *chicken breasts*

polenta

spinach

orange

garlic

thyme

1 To make the marinade, strip the lavender flowers from the stems and combine with the orange zest, garlic, honey and salt. Add the olive oil and herbs. Slash the chicken deeply, spread the mixture over the chicken and leave to marinate in a cool place for at least 20 minutes.

2 To make the polenta, bring the chicken stock to the boil in a heavy saucepan. Add the corn meal in a steady stream, stirring all the time until thick: this will take 2–3 minutes. Turn the cooked polenta out on to a 2.5-cm/1-in-deep buttered tray and allow to cool.

3 Heat the grill (broiler) to a moderate temperature. (If using a barbecue, let the embers settle to a steady glow.) Grill (broil) the chicken for about 15 minutes, turning once.

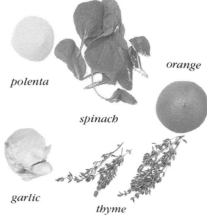

4 Cut the polenta into 2.5 cm/1 in cubes with a wet knife. Heat the butter in a large frying-pan (skillet) and fry the polenta until golden.

COOK'S TIP

Lavender marinade is a delicious
flavouring for salt-water fish as well as
chicken. Try it over grilled cod,
haddock, halibut, sea bass and bream.

5 Wash the salad leaves and spin dry,
then divide between 4 large plates. Slice
each chicken breast and lay over the
salad. Place the polenta among the
salad, decorate with sprigs of lavender and
tomatoes, season and serve.

Millionaire's Lobster Salad

When money is no object and you're in a decadent mood, this salad will satisfy your every whim. It is ideally served with a cool Chardonnay, Chablis or Pouilly-Fuissé wine.

Serves 4

INGREDIENTS
1 medium lobster, live or cooked
salt
1 bay leaf
1 sprig thyme
700 g/1½ lb new potatoes, scrubbed
2 ripe tomatoes
4 oranges
½ frisée lettuce
175 g/6 oz lamb's lettuce
60 ml/4 tbsp extra-virgin olive oil
200 g/7 oz can young artichokes in brine, quartered
1 small bunch tarragon, chervil or flat-leaf parsley

DRESSING
30 ml/2 tbsp frozen concentrated orange juice, thawed
75 g/3 oz unsalted butter, diced
salt and cayenne pepper

COOK'S TIP

The rich delicate flavour of this salad depends on using the freshest lobsters. If North Atlantic lobsters (pictured here) are not available, use spiny rock lobsters or crawfish.

new potatoes

lamb's lettuce　*lobster*

orange

tarragon

tomato

frisée lettuce

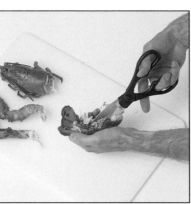

1 If the lobster needs cooking, add to a large pan of salted water with the bay leaf and thyme. Bring to the boil and simmer for 15 minutes. Cool under running water. Twist off the legs and claws, and separate the tail piece from the body section. Break the claws open with a hammer and remove the meat intact. Cut the tail piece open from the underside with a pair of kitchen shears. Slice the meat and set aside.

2 Bring the potatoes to the boil in salted water and simmer for 20 minutes. Drain, cover and keep warm. Cover the tomatoes with boiling water and leave for 20 seconds to loosen their skins. Cool under running water and slip off the skins. Halve the tomatoes, discard the seeds, then cut the flesh into large dice.

3 To segment the oranges, remove the peel from the top, bottom and sides with a serrated knife. With a small paring knife, loosen the orange segments by cutting between the flesh and the membranes, holding the fruit over a small bowl.

4 To make the dressing, measure the thawed orange juice into a glass bowl and set it over a saucepan containing 2.5 cm/1 in of simmering water. Heat the juice for 1 minute, remove from the heat, then whisk in the butter a little at a time until the dressing reaches a coating consistency. Season to taste with salt and a pinch of cayenne pepper, cover and keep warm.

5 Wash the salad leaves and spin dry. Dress with olive oil, then divide between 4 large serving plates. Moisten the potatoes, artichokes and orange segments with olive oil and distribute among the leaves. Lay the sliced lobster over the salad, spoon on the warm butter dressing, add the diced tomato and decorate with fresh herbs. Serve at room temperature.

Warm Duck Salad with Orange and Coriander

The rich gamey flavour of duck provides the foundation for this delicious salad. Serve it in late summer or autumn and enjoy the warm flavour of orange and coriander.

Serves 4

INGREDIENTS
1 small orange
2 boneless duck breasts
150 ml/5 fl oz/⅔ cup dry white wine
5 ml/1 tsp ground coriander seeds
½ tsp ground cumin or fennel seeds
30 ml/2 tbsp caster (superfine) sugar
juice of ½ small lime or lemon
salt and cayenne pepper
75 g/3 oz day-old bread, thickly sliced
45 ml/3 tbsp garlic oil (see Introduction)
½ escarole lettuce
½ frisée lettuce
30 ml/2 tbsp sunflower or groundnut oil
4 sprigs fresh coriander

1 Halve the orange and slice thickly. Discard any stray pips and place the slices in a small saucepan. Cover with water, bring to the boil and simmer for 5 minutes to remove the bitterness. Drain and set aside.

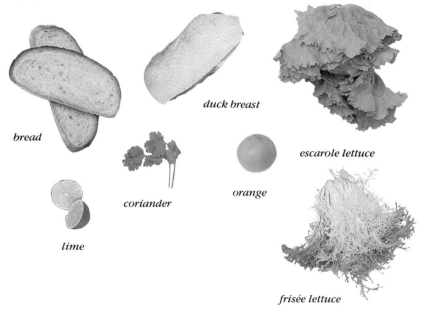

bread

duck breast

coriander

lime

orange

escarole lettuce

frisée lettuce

2 Pierce the skin of the duck breasts diagonally with a small knife (this will help release the fat as they cook). Rub the skin with salt. Place a steel or cast-iron frying-pan (skillet) over a steady heat and cook the breasts for 20 minutes, turning once, until they are medium-rare. Transfer to a warm plate, cover and keep warm. Pour the duck fat into a small bowl and set aside for use on another occasion.

3 Heat the sediment in the frying-pan until it begins to darken and caramelize. Add the wine and stir to loosen the sediment. Add the ground coriander, cumin, sugar and orange slices. Boil quickly and reduce to a coating consistency. Sharpen with lime juice and season to taste with salt and cayenne pepper. Transfer to a bowl, cover and keep warm.

4 To make the garlic croûtons, remove the crusts from the bread and discard them. Cut the bread into short fingers. Heat the garlic oil in a heavy frying-pan and brown until evenly crisp. Season with salt, then turn out on to kitchen paper (paper towels).

5 Wash the salad leaves and spin dry. Moisten with sunflower oil and distribute between 4 large serving plates.

6 Slice the duck breasts diagonally with a carving knife. Divide the breast meat into 4 and lift on to each salad plate. Spoon on the dressing, scatter with croûtons, decorate with a sprig of coriander and serve.

COOK'S TIP
Duck breast has the quality of red meat and is cooked either rare, medium or well done according to taste.

Blueberry, Orange and Lavender Salad

Delicate blueberries emerge here in a simple salad of sharp oranges and little meringues flavoured with lavender.

Serves 4

INGREDIENTS
6 oranges
350 g/12 oz blueberries
8 sprigs fresh lavender

MERINGUE
2 egg whites
125 g/4 oz/½ cup caster (superfine) sugar
5 ml/1 tsp fresh lavender flowers

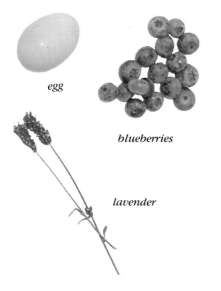

egg

blueberries

lavender

orange

1 Pre-heat the oven to 140°C/275°F/ Gas mark 1. Line a baking tray (sheet) with 6 layers of newspaper and cover with non-stick baking parchment. Whisk the egg whites in a large mixing bowl until they hold their weight on the whisk. Add the sugar a little at a time, whisking thoroughly before each addition. Fold in the lavender flowers.

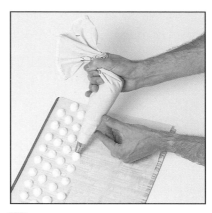

2 Spoon the meringue into a piping bag fitted with a 6 mm/¼ in plain nozzle. Pipe as many small buttons of meringue on to the prepared baking-sheet as you can. Dry the meringue near the bottom of the oven for 1½–2 hours.

3 To segment the oranges, remove the peel from the top, bottom and sides with a serrated knife. Loosen the segments by cutting with a paring knife between the flesh and the membranes, holding the fruit over a bowl.

4 Arrange the segments on 4 plates.

5 Combine the blueberries with the lavender meringues and pile in the centre of each plate. Decorate with sprigs of lavender and serve.

COOK'S TIP

Lavender is used in both sweet and savoury dishes. Always use fresh or recently dried flowers, and avoid artificially scented bunches that are sold for domestic purposes.

Blackberry Salad with Rose Granita

The blackberry is a member of the rose family and combines especially well with rose water. Here a rose syrup is frozen into a granita and served over strips of white meringue.

COOK'S TIP

Blackberries are widely cultivated from late spring to autumn and are usually large, plump and sweet. The finest berries have a bitter edge and a strong depth of flavour – best appreciated with a sprinkling of sugar.

Serves 4

INGREDIENTS
150 g/5 oz/²/₃ cup caster (superfine) sugar
1 fresh red rose, petals finely chopped
5 ml/1 tsp rose water
10 ml/2 tsp lemon juice
450 g/1 lb blackberries
icing (confectioners') sugar, for dusting

MERINGUE
2 egg whites
125 g/4 oz/½ cup caster sugar

eggs

blackberries

rose

1 Bring 150 ml/5 fl oz/²/₃ cup water to the boil in a stainless-steel or enamel saucepan. Add the sugar and rose petals, then simmer for 5 minutes. Strain the syrup into a deep metal tray, add a further 450 ml/15 fl oz/scant 2 cups water, the rose water and lemon juice, and leave to cool. Freeze the mixture for 3 hours or until solid.

2 Pre-heat the oven to 140°C/275°F/ Gas mark 1. Line a baking tray (sheet) with 6 layers of newspaper and cover with non-stick baking parchment.

3 For the meringue, whisk the egg whites until they hold their weight on the whisk. Add the caster sugar a little at a time and whisk until firm.

4 Spoon the meringue into a piping bag fitted with a 1 cm/½ in plain nozzle. Pipe the meringue in lengths across the paper-lined baking-sheet. Dry in the bottom of the oven for 1½–2 hours.

5 Break the meringue into 5 cm/2 in lengths and place 3 or 4 lengths on each of 4 large plates. Pile the blackberries next to the meringue. With a tablespoon, scrape the granita finely. Shape into ovals and place over the meringue. Dust with icing sugar and serve.

Raspberry Salad with Mango Custard Sauce

This remarkable salad unites the sharp quality of fresh raspberries with a special custard made from rich fragrant mangoes.

Serves 4

INGREDIENTS
1 large mango
3 egg yolks
30 ml/2 tbsp caster (superfine) sugar
10 ml/2 tsp cornflour (cornstarch)
200 ml/7 fl oz/scant 1 cup milk
8 sprigs fresh mint

RASPBERRY SAUCE
500 g/1 lb 2 oz raspberries
45 ml/3 tbsp caster sugar

eggs

mint

mango

raspberries

1 To prepare the mango, remove the top and bottom with a serrated knife. Cut away the outer skin, then remove the flesh by cutting either side of the flat central stone. Save one half of the fruit for decoration and roughly chop the remainder.

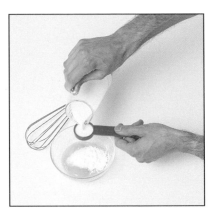

2 For the custard, combine the egg yolks, sugar, cornflour and 30 ml/2 tbsp of the milk smoothly in a bowl.

3 Rinse a small saucepan out with cold water to prevent the milk from catching. Bring the rest of the milk to the boil in the pan, pour it over the ingredients in the bowl and stir evenly.

4 Sieve the mixture back into the saucepan, stir to a simmer and allow the mixture to thicken.

5 Pour the custard into a food processor, add the chopped mango and blend until smooth. Allow to cool.

COOK'S TIP

Mangoes are ripe when they yield to gentle pressure in the hand. Some varieties show a red-gold or yellow flush when they are ready to eat.

6 To make the raspberry sauce, place 350 g/12 oz of the raspberries in a stain-resistant saucepan. Add the sugar, soften over a gentle heat and simmer for 5 minutes. Rub the fruit through a fine nylon sieve to remove the seeds. Allow to cool.

7 Spoon the raspberry sauce and mango custard into 2 pools on 4 plates. Slice the reserved mango and fan out or arrange in a pattern over the raspberry sauce. Scatter fresh raspberries over the mango custard. Decorate with 2 sprigs of mint and serve.

Iced Pineapple Crush with Strawberries and Lychees

The sweet tropical flavours of pineapple and lychees combine well with richly scented strawberries to make this a most refreshing salad.

Serves 4

INGREDIENTS
2 small pineapples
450 g/1 lb strawberries
400 g/14 oz can lychees
45 ml/3 tbsp kirsch or white rum
30 ml/2 tbsp icing (confectioners')
   sugar

pineapple

strawberries

1 Remove the crown from both pineapples by twisting sharply. Reserve the leaves for decoration.

2 Cut the fruit in half diagonally with a large serrated knife.

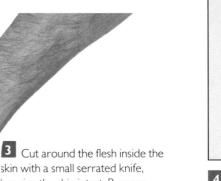

3 Cut around the flesh inside the skin with a small serrated knife, keeping the skin intact. Remove the core from the pineapple.

4 Chop the pineapple and combine with the strawberries and lychees, taking care not to damage the fruit.

COOK'S TIP

A ripe pineapple will resist pressure when squeezed and will have a sweet, fragrant smell. In winter freezing conditions can cause the flesh to blacken.

5 Combine the kirsch with the icing sugar, pour over the fruit and freeze for 45 minutes.

6 Turn the fruit out into the pineapple skins and decorate with pineapple leaves.

Fresh Fig, Apple and Date Salad

Sweet Mediterranean figs and dates combine especially well with crisp dessert apples. A hint of almond serves to unite the flavours.

Serves 4

INGREDIENTS
6 large apples
juice of ½ lemon
175 g/6 oz fresh dates
25 g/1 oz white marzipan
5 ml/1 tsp orange flower water
60 ml/4 tbsp natural (plain) yogurt
4 green or purple figs
4 almonds, toasted

apples

figs

almonds

dates

1 Core the apples. Slice thinly, then cut into fine matchsticks. Moisten with lemon juice to keep them white.

2 Remove the stones (pits) from the dates and cut the flesh into fine strips, then combine with the apple slices.

3 Soften the marzipan with orange flower water and combine with the yogurt. Mix well.

4 Pile the apples and dates in the centre of 4 plates. Remove the stem from each of the figs and divide the fruit into quarters without cutting right through the base. Squeeze the base with the thumb and forefinger of each hand to open up the fruit.

5 Place a fig in the centre of the salad, spoon in the yogurt filling and decorate with a toasted almond.

Muscat Grape Frappé

The flavour and perfume of the Muscat grape is rarely more enticing than when captured in this icy-cool salad. Because of its alcohol content this dish is not suitable for young children.

Serves 4

INGREDIENTS
½ bottle Muscat wine, Beaumes de
   Venise, Frontignan or Rivsaltes
450 g/1 lb Muscat grapes

Muscat wine

Muscat grapes

1 Pour the wine into a stainless-steel or enamel tray, add 150 ml/5 fl oz/⅔ cup water and freeze for 3 hours or until completely solid.

2 Remove the seeds from the grapes with a pair of tweezers. If you have time, peel the grapes.

3 Scrape the frozen wine with a tablespoon to make a fine ice. Combine the grapes with the ice and spoon into 4 shallow glasses.

Grapefruit Salad with Campari and Orange

The bitter-sweet flavour of Campari combines especially well with citrus fruit. Because of its alcohol content, this dish is not suitable for young children.

Serves 4

INGREDIENTS
45 ml/3 tbsp caster (superfine) sugar
60 ml/4 tbsp Campari
30 ml/2 tbsp lemon juice
4 grapefruit
5 oranges
4 sprigs fresh mint

COOK'S TIP
When buying citrus fruit, choose brightly coloured varieties that feel heavy for their size.

grapefruit

oranges

mint

lemon juice

Campari

1 Bring 150 ml/5 fl oz/⅔ cup water to the boil in a small saucepan, add the sugar and simmer until dissolved. Cool in a metal tray, then add the Campari and lemon juice. Chill until ready to serve.

2 Cut the peel from the top, bottom and sides of the grapefruit and oranges with a serrated knife. Segment the fruit into a bowl by slipping a small paring knife between the flesh and the membranes. Combine the fruit with the Campari syrup and chill.

3 Spoon the salad into 4 dishes and finish with a sprig of fresh mint.

91

Strawberries with Raspberry and Passion Fruit Sauce

Fragrant strawberries release their finest flavour when moistened with a sauce of fresh raspberries and scented passion fruit.

Serves 4

INGREDIENTS

350 g/12 oz raspberries, fresh or frozen
45 ml/3 tbsp caster (superfine) sugar
1 passion fruit
700 g/1½ lb small strawberries
8 plain finger biscuits (butter cookies), to serve

biscuits (cookies)

raspberries

passion fruit

strawberries

1 Place the raspberries and sugar into a stain-resistant saucepan and soften over a gentle heat to release the juices. Simmer for 5 minutes. Allow to cool.

2 Halve the passion fruit and scoop out the seeds and juice.

3 Turn the raspberries into a food processor or blender, add the passion fruit and blend smoothly.

COOK'S TIP

Berry fruits offer their best flavour when served at room temperature.

4 Pass the fruit sauce through a fine nylon sieve to remove the seeds.

5 Fold the strawberries into the sauce, then spoon into 4 stemmed glasses. Serve with plain finger biscuits (butter cookies).

Mixed Melon Salad with Wild Strawberries

Ice-cold melon is a delicious way to end a meal. Here several varieties are combined with strongly flavoured wild or woodland strawberries. If wild berries are not available, use ordinary strawberries or raspberries.

Serves 4

INGREDIENTS
1 cantaloupe or charentais melon
1 galia melon
900 g/2 lb water melon
175 g/6 oz wild strawberries
4 sprigs fresh mint

wild strawberries

galia melon

mint

cantaloupe melon

water melon

COOK'S TIP
Ripe melons should give slightly when pressed at the base, and should give off a fruity, melony scent. Buy carefully if you plan to use the fruit on the day.

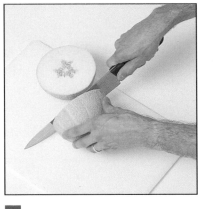

1 Halve the cantaloupe, galia and water melons.

2 Remove the seeds from the cantaloupe and galia with a spoon.

3 With a melon scoop, take out as many balls as you can from all 3 melons. Combine in a large bowl and refrigerate.

4 Add the wild strawberries and turn out into 4 stemmed glass dishes.

5 Decorate with sprigs of mint.

INDEX